Town
Gardening

JOHN C. DALE

Town Gardening

EBURY PRESS
LONDON

To Betsy and Raymond, my mother and father,
who were both keen amateur gardeners and
encouraged me in the early days.

Published by Ebury Press
National Magazine House
72 Broadwick Street
London W1V 2BP

© John C Dale and The National Magazine Co Ltd 1980

ISBN 0 85223 173 3

Designed by Derek Morrison
Line drawings and plans by Janet Sparrow
Cover photograph by Harry Smith

Filmset in Great Britain by
Advanced Filmsetters (Glasgow) Ltd
Printed by Cambridge University Press, Cambridge
Bound by Hazell Watson & Viney Ltd, Aylesbury

Contents

Foreword

I have written this book especially for you, the town gardener. Bricks and concrete surround you; the air is polluted; you have to contend with lack of light, poor, worked-out soil and a shortage of space, and you may well feel that under such conditions creating a garden is impossible.

But *it can be done*. If you examine your property closely the chances are that you will find it has much greater potential than you thought.

Regardless of how diminutive or difficult your space may be, it can still be transformed into a tiny piece of the country with its own unique characteristics, and you will be able to enjoy that particular sense of achievement that comes from growing things of beauty in such unpromising surroundings. Furthermore an attractive garden will do much to improve the value of your property.

You don't need to spend a great deal of money. The work can cost as little or as much as you wish. Naturally, some plants may appear a trifle expensive in the first instance, but bear in mind that many of them will provide infinite pleasure for years to come.

This book contains advice based upon my own many years of practical experience in the creation and maintenance of town gardens. It is designed to help you turn your dream garden into a reality, and I hope that you will enjoy reading it as much as I have enjoyed writing it.

John C. Dale

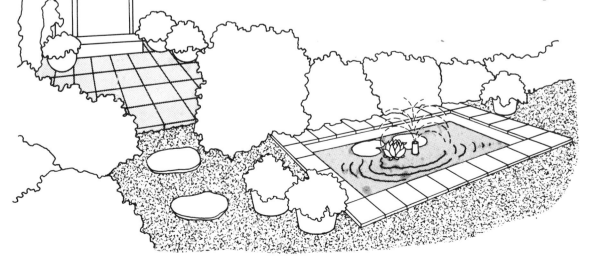

It is the wisdom and goodness of gardening which makes it such a deep and enduring happiness. It is thankfulness, reverence, and love, which make our gardens dear to us from childhood to old age.

Dean Hole, *In Nature's Garden*

Designing Your Garden

If you plan your design in too much of a hurry you may later come to regret it. People often look for ways of avoiding the work of initial construction when in fact they should be more concerned about reducing the amount of maintenance involved once the garden has been established. If the job is to be done successfully then it must be tackled properly right from the start.

First of all, analyse your assets and handicaps. Look at the garden, courtyard or back yard from the windows of the house and then consider what the house looks like from the garden. Pay particular attention to any surrounding walls, gate posts and balconies. Evaluate the view beyond the garden area itself:

> Are there any high buildings close by?
> Is the site enclosed on all sides, or does it have an open outlook in one or more directions?
> How does the view affect you? Is it depressing, because of some unsightly building or a factory nearby?
> Or is there an attractive tree or pretty summerhouse in your neighbour's garden that you wouldn't want to obscure?

All reactions to such questions need to be taken into account in the planning stage.

Draw the site

The next thing is to make a drawing of the site. Measure it with care and draw a scale plan on squared paper. Note any special features such as shrubs or trees, and any noticeable changes in ground level, so that these factors may be used to advantage in your final design. Plot the position of any existing paths and paved areas, and the space occupied by anything else – the storage tank for oil, coal bunker, dustbins. Note any drainage gullies and inspection chamber covers. Finally, make brief notes about the surrounding view and indicate the four points of the compass.

Things to bear in mind

When looking for suitable design solutions for a confined area it is always wise to keep the centre free from clutter and to place any new special features a little to one side or towards one end. This creates the illusion of more space. On small sites surrounded by a high wall it is as well to forget about a lawn because it is never going to be much of a success. A better

1 Design for an L-shaped garden

Garden area approximately 200 sq m (roughly 2153 sq ft)

An imaginative use of an L-shaped area, making the most of its double aspect; the sun dial (10) placed off-centre, on a diagonal line between the outer corner of the house and the shrub border (2) opposite it, becomes a focus, and the stepping stones (12), set across the narrow foot of the L, give an illusion of greater breadth.

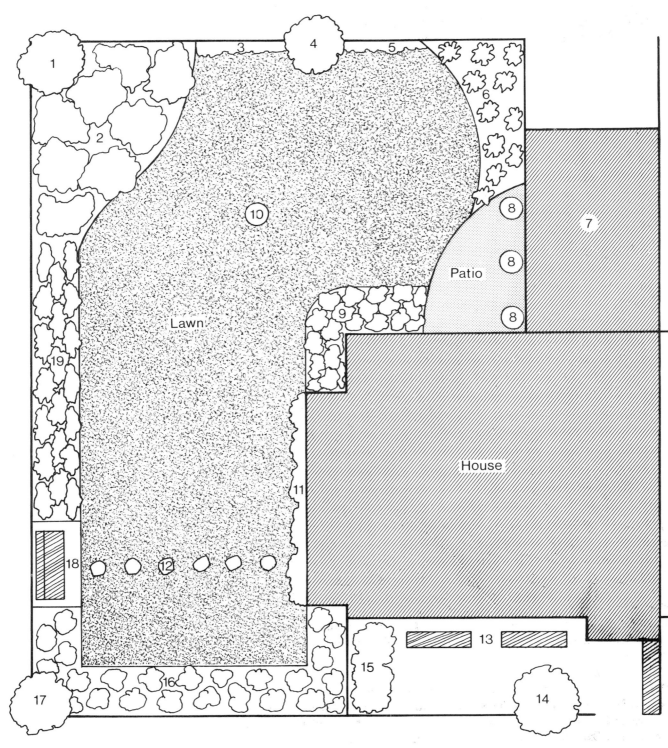

alternative is to pave the site and introduce raised beds about 45 cm (18 in) high so that the plants in them will get more of the available light and will be easier to tend by anyone who is elderly or disabled. In high rainfall areas it is always advisable to use raised beds to improve drainage. If you feel you must have a patch of grass then consider putting down one of the artificial grass surfaces. This will be expensive but at least it will need little or no maintenance.

Next consider what, if any, new structures are to be added, such as a garden shed, summer-house or greenhouse. If one of these is already on the site is it located in the most suitable place? If there are paths and other hard surfaces, what is their state of repair? Boundary walls may be in a tumble-down state, or they may need some pointing-up, or they may be perfect. Go out and make a detailed inspection of all these items. It's no use planting climbers against walls which are in a poor state because any repair work later on will create havoc among the climbers.

Be sure to install a tap to which you can attach a garden hose, and remember that an additional water rate will be payable for it.

When your garden is a going concern you will need to dispose of the week-by-week debris, and dustmen generally refuse to accept it. You can put soft growth such as lawn mowings and leaves into a compost heap, so plan to have one in a well-screened spot. Hedge trimmings and other woody material can be taken away (perhaps by arrangement with the local garden club) or put on a bonfire. Choose the site for your hearth or incinerator with care, as far away as possible from your neighbours' windows. When you light a fire the material should be dry enough not to produce heavy smoke, and you should avoid windy days or days when your neighbours are drying the washing or having a party.

Try out alternative designs

Put a piece of tracing paper over your original drawing of the site and plot on this some of the features you would like to introduce. Remember what assets and handicaps you noted before. One or more of them may contribute something helpful either architecturally or horticulturally to the final design.

Carefully consider the specimen designs in this book (see diagrams 1–6). One of them may fit your needs perfectly, or perhaps you would prefer to incorporate features from several different designs.

Make a short list of what you would like to include if space will permit, and work out an order of priorities. A sitting-out area may be top of the list, in which case you will need to earmark the sunniest corner. You may also need a utility area for hanging out washing from time to time. Other features you may want to include are a patio, pond, rose beds, herbaceous border, shrub border and so on. Try incorporating these

---

KEY TO DIAGRAM 1

1 *Cotoneaster* 'Hybridus pendulus' 2 Shrub border 3 *Cotoneaster lacteus* 4 *Magnolia liliflora* 5 *Actinidia kolomikta* 6 Border of slow growing dwarf conifers 7 Flat-roofed garage with potential as a roof garden 8 Hanging baskets 9 Spring and summer bedding displays 10 Sun dial 11 *Hydrangea petiolaris* 12 Stepping stones set in the lawn 13 Flower boxes for the spring and summer bedding display 14 *Laburnum* 'Vossii' 15 *Elaeagnus pungens* 'Maculata' 16 Rose border 17 *Sorbus aria* 'Chrysophylla' 18 Garden seat 19 Herbaceous border.

2 An easily maintained design for a typical town garden

Garden area approximately 200 sq m (roughly 2153 sq ft)
19 m by 10 m (62 ft by 34 ft)

The problem posed by this site is how to broaden its apparent width. The solution has been achieved in this design by carrying the patio right across directly behind the house and adopting the device of a sweeping curve. The curve, a gravel path (3), is continued to the far boundary, leading the eye to a lily pool (6) on the right and a ginkgo (11) set against a crescent of shrubs (12) on the left. A sculptured figure (10) is the focal point.

KEY TO DIAGRAM 2

1 Bucket type plant containers **2** Flower borders **3** Gravel path **4** Stone plant containers **5** Crazy paving **6** Lily pool **7** Wisteria **8** Area for bonfire and compost heap **9** Garden seat (movable) **10** Sculptured figure **11** *Ginkgo biloba* **12** Mixed shrubs **13** Clematis

---

various ideas on successive pieces of tracing paper. Even consider removing existing paths and constructing new ones in more satisfactory places. The same goes for existing trees and shrubs. You may want to raise or lower the level of part of your site or to establish a lawn where none existed before.

Anything is possible on paper. Examine each and every possible combination of the various factors until you reach a design which is both aesthetically satisfying and practicable.

Back to reality

Now come down from the clouds and cast a cold realistic eye on the site as it is at present. It may well be neglected, covered with masses of weeds and brambles, with perhaps an old rockery that has gone to ruin. A great deal of physical labour is involved in tackling a run-down or neglected garden. Manual labour is an acquired skill and those who are not used to it would be well advised to take things easy and not try to accomplish too much too soon. The emphasis should be on 'little and often'. Friends may give you a hand with the more arduous work, or alternatively, if you can afford to do so, you could put the whole of the work out to contract (see pages 123–127 for more information).

Clearing your site

Even if the site is badly neglected, Dalapon can be used to kill couch grass and all the other grass-type weeds, and ammonium sulphate (Amcide) will eradicate weeds, small trees and brushwood.

Make time to read the instructions on the containers before employing weedkillers, follow them scrupulously and keep them well away from children, old people whose sight may be failing and from animals. All spraying should be undertaken on a still day for the spray can cause serious trouble with your neighbours if their plants are destroyed due to your neglect.

Do read the next three chapters, which go into more detail about the problems you may encounter, before you begin to make any physical alterations to your garden.

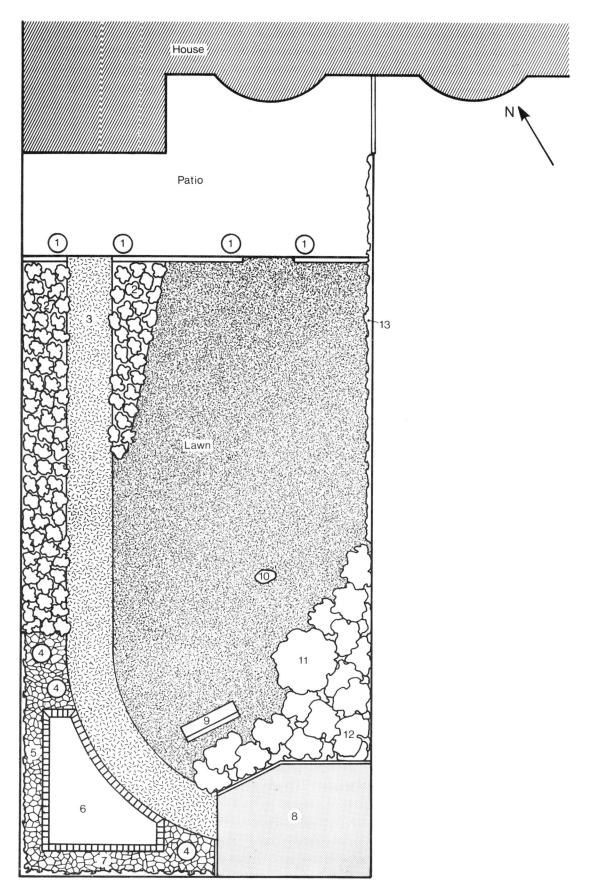

House

Patio

N

13

3 Design for a medium-sized walled terrace garden

Garden area approximately 163 sq m (roughly 1754 sq ft)
16.75 m by 9.75 m (55 ft by 31 ft)

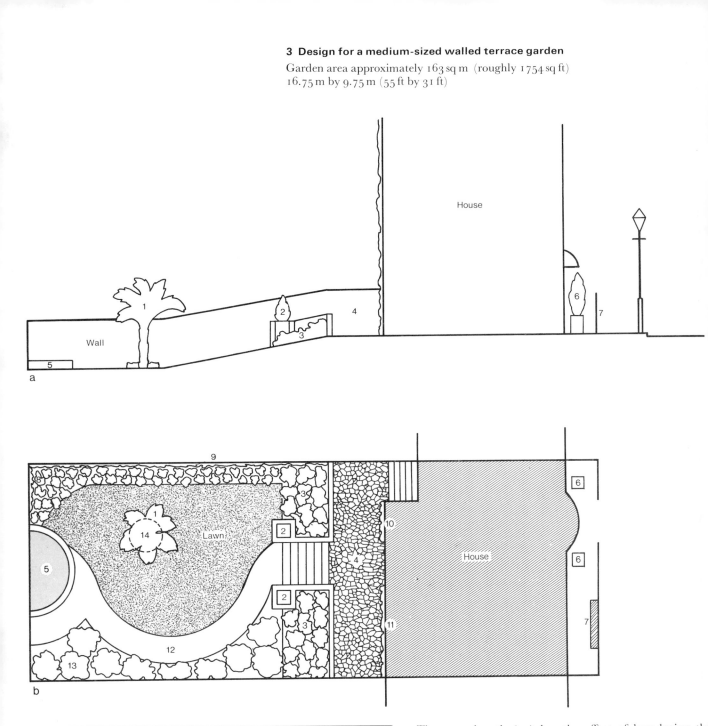

KEY TO DIAGRAM 3

1 *Trachycarpus fortunei* **2** *Taxus baccata* 'Fastigiata' **3** *Cotoneaster horizontalis* 'Variegatus' **4** Paved terrace **5** Lily pond **6** *Laurus nobilis* (bay tree in tub or other plant container) **7** Frontage providing suitable site for flower boxes for spring and summer display **8** Border for spring and summer bedding **9** *Hedera colchica dentata* 'Aurea' **10** *Solanum crispum autumnale* **11** Clematis 'Lasurstern. **12** Path **13** Border for flowering shrubs

The curved path (12) has the effect of broadening th garden, and the palm (1), used as a focal point, is placed o centre opposite the widest part of the curve to further th illusion. The Chusan palm, *Trachycarpus fortunei*, is hard enough to grow quite successfully in the south and west Britain and elsewhere in sheltered places. A bay tree, *Laur. nobilis* (6), adds interest at the front of the house whic would also be a suitable place for window boxes.

4 Design for a squarish walled garden

Garden area approximately 167 sq m (roughly 1798 sq ft)
12.20 m by 13.70 m (40 ft by 45 ft)

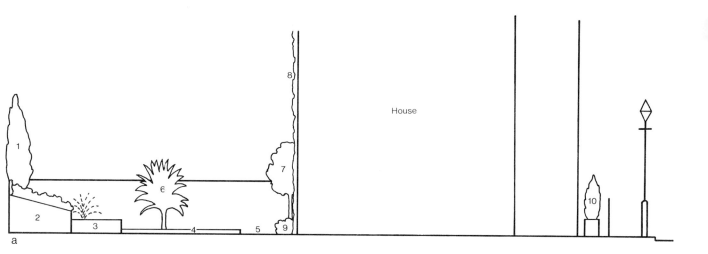

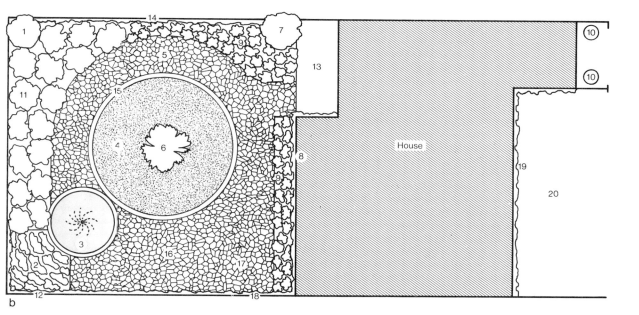

The aim here is to create a vista within a confined space, an effect aided by
placing a fountain (3) just beyond and to the left of the circular lawn (4),
behind which the rising slope of the heather garden (2) and shrub border
(11) provide a backcloth. The curved sweep of the path (5) complements the
curve of the lawn in which is a small cabbage palm, *Cordyline australis* (6),
which forms an exotic focal point.

5 A simple, easily maintained garden for a house with a basement

Garden area approximately 127 sq m (roughly 1357 sq ft)
16.75 m by 7.6 m (55 ft by 25 ft)

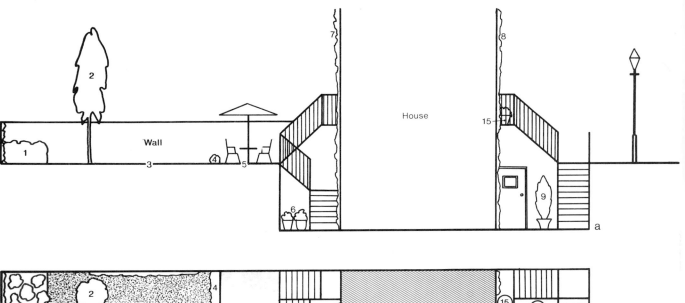

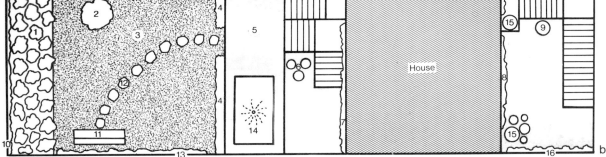

KEY TO DIAGRAM 5
1 Mixed floribunda roses
2 *Eucalyptus gunnii*
3 Lawn
4 Flower borders
5 Patio
6 Plant containers
7 *Parthenocissus henryana*
8 *Jasminum officinale* 'Grandiflorum'
9 *Chamaecyparis lawsoniana*
10 *Hedera canariensis* 'Variegata'
11 Garden bench
12 Stepping stones set in the lawn
13 *Clematis montana rubens*
14 Water feature with fountain and underwater lighting
15 Containers for spring and summer bedding
16 *Lonicera japonica* 'Halliana'

Typical of the gardens of many town houses built before 1914, this is a longish, narrow plot which has been designed to minimize its defects. The plan is labour saving and provides plenty of space for outdoor living; the fountain (14) and underwater lighting give interest to the sitting out area, making it particularly pleasant on summer evenings.

6 Design for a very long, narrow garden

Garden area approximately 126 sq m (roughly 1536 sq ft)
18.30 m by 6.90 m (60 ft by 23 ft)

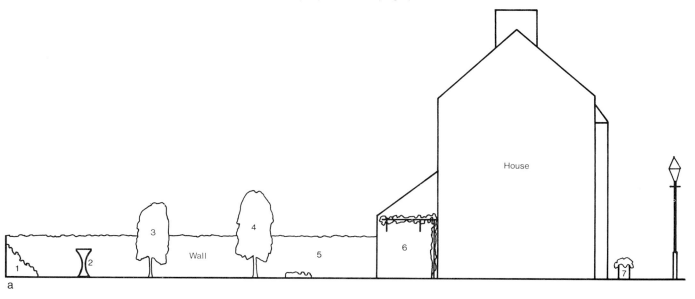

a

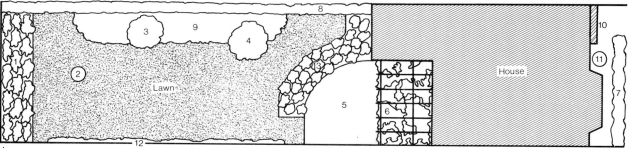

b

KEY TO DIAGRAM 6

1 Herbaceous border
2 Bird bath
3 *Acer palmatum dissectum*
4 *Betula pendula* 'Youngii'
5 Sheltered patio, bounded by flower border
6 Arbour formed in an angle of the back of the house, with climbing roses
7 Low earth-filled wall planted with *Picea pungens* 'Procumbens' and *Hedera helix* 'Buttercup'
8 Hedge of *Cupressocyparis leylandii*
9 Ground cover planting of *Vinca minor*, with daffodils naturalized amidst the roots, and crocuses
10 Suitable site for a hanging basket
11 Container for spring and summer bedding
12 *Forsythia suspensa* clothing the wall
13 Flower border for spring and summer bedding

To create an illusion of greater breadth, the flower border (13) cuts a boldly sweeping curve across the garden close to the house, following the curve of the patio (5). At the sides, conventional flower beds have been avoided so as to take the lawn as close to the boundaries as possible, and the line of the hedge (8) is interrupted by two specimen trees (3, 4) growing among crocuses and daffodils, in spring.

Grass Roots

To succeed with the cultivation of plants, shrubs and trees you really do need to understand the nature of the soil in which they grow. Of course success is further influenced by such factors as light and shade and sheltered or exposed situations, but most important is getting to know your own garden soil and finding out what if anything you can do to improve its quality.

Understanding Your Soil Type

Soil is a complex substance which has taken millions of years to evolve. It is a collection of rock particles, some large, some very small, plus a variable amount of organic matter. It also contains water, air and masses of living organisms, many of which are so infinitesimally small that they cannot be seen with the naked eye. Yet unless they are present the soil will become a dead substance, incapable of supporting any form of plant life. It is a comforting thought that a soil which is capable of supporting weeds will also support more desirable plants.

Humus: the organic key to fertility
In nature soil fertility is self-renewing. Countless generations of plants and animals live and die and finally become part of the earth from which they came, to help support future generations of plants and animals (see diagrams 7a and 7b). All good soils contain this organic matter, or 'humus'. You can make your own garden soil richer in humus by adding manure, compost, peat, seaweed, and similar materials. Humus is essential because:

> It provides plant food.
> It maintains the vast population of micro-organisms in the soil.
> It improves soil structure.
> It improves drainage in heavy soils and water-holding properties in sandy soils.

The three types of soil
The first thing you need to know about the soil in your garden is the physical type (see diagram 8).

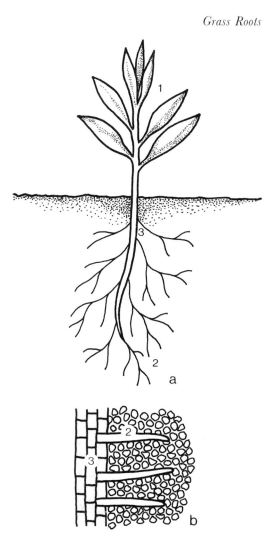

a

b

7 The plant 'factory'

a The foliage (**1**) takes carbon dioxide from the air and simple substances dissolved in water from the soil, turns them into carbohydrates, proteins and fats and releases water and oxygen. Root hairs (**2**) take dissolved mineral nutrients from around the soil particles and these are transported through the tap root (**3**) to the foliage.

b The root hairs magnified: single, elongated cells (**2**) growing from the tap root (**3**) push their way between the soil particles.

Heavy soils contain an excess of the smaller rock particles which make up clay. Such soils are badly drained and low in humus, soil organisms and air. They are 'cold' soils, late to warm up in spring, so that plants get away to a bad start and growth is somewhat retarded.

Sandy soils are just the opposite. They have an excess of the larger rock particles and a low humus content. Soil organisms are also less in evidence, for there is nothing much for them to live on. Sandy soils warm up early in spring due to the relatively large air spaces between the particles. They are excessively well drained, and rain quickly washes nutrients down into the subsoil beyond the reach of many plants, so sandy soils are starved soils.

The ideal soil is midway between these two extremes, and is called a

1

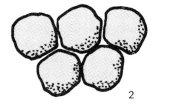

2

3

8 Physical types of soil

Heavy clay soils are cold and wet because they contain an excess of small rock particles (**1**) and the smaller the size of the particle the greater the relative surface area (**3**) for retaining moisture.
Light sandy soils have an excess of coarse sand particles (**2**) with larger air spaces between, which means that they have poorer moisture-holding capacity.

medium loam. It has enough of the coarser and finer rock particles to overcome the bad qualities associated with each, together with sufficient humus to hold onto the necessary amount of moisture. Such a soil is able to support the large number of living organisms which are so very important for fertility. It is said to be 'in balance' because it is able to maintain its structure and texture over long periods of time, and plants flourish in it.

Improving soil texture

Heavy clay soils can be improved by the incorporation of coarse sand, peat, or, if you live in an area where this is available, coke breeze, which is ash from a power house. Where it can be obtained 'long manure' is still the best material to use. This is manure with much undecomposed straw in it and it should be applied in autumn and thoroughly incorporated into the top spade's depth of soil. It should never be applied in spring for it will be a long time decomposing and will more than likely dry out the soil.

Sandy soils are very dry, hungry soils and they need regular applications of bulky organic matter such as cow manure, vegetable compost, decomposed lawn mowings, peat or seaweed. These help to bind together the particles in the soil, giving it greater moisture-holding capacity and thus the plants in it greater drought resistance. Minerals are less easily washed down into the subsoil, and the anchorage of plant roots is improved, which means that those plants in exposed positions are less easily disturbed.

Chemical Fertilizers

The physical structure and texture of your soil is important, but equally important are the chemicals in it. Plants need many different chemicals if they are to grow properly, and though most of these are present in almost any soil there are four which are needed in quantity by plant life and which are often in short supply. These are nitrogen, phosphate, potash and lime (see diagram 9).

Nitrogen, phosphate and potash

Nitrogen stimulates plant growth. It improves the quantity and quality of the foliage. When applied to the ground in a readily available form it has a noticeable effect in a matter of days.

Phosphate is particularly important for stimulating the early growth of seedlings and in general improves root development and brings about earlier maturity.

Potash has a steadying effect over the rank growth which would be the result of an excessive supply of nitrogen. So remember that if you are using regular light applications of a nitrogenous fertilizer it is necessary to balance this by increasing the supply of potash. Potash also helps to harden growth which would otherwise be too soft and lush when stimulated by nitrogen alone, thus making it less susceptible to fungus diseases. It improves the colour of flowers and fruit and reduces the loss of water from plants, an important effect when you are gardening on sandy soil or in an area of low rainfall.

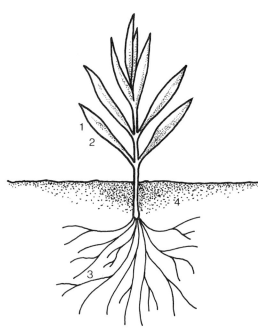

9 The four essential fertilizers
1 Nitrogen to stimulate growth of foliage
2 Potash to balance the nitrogen
3 Phosphate to improve root development
4 Lime to reduce soil acidity—among other functions

Lime: the chemical key to fertility

Lime is present in the soil in the form of calcium which is a constituent of most plants and naturally, as plants live off the soil, reserves of this element are gradually reduced. If soil is short of lime it is said to be 'acid'; if it is naturally calcareous or over-limed it is called 'alkaline'.

Lime encourages the activities of the organisms which break down organic matter into humus, but lime alone is not enough. If you keep on applying it without adding suitable dressings of organic matter this will in fact lead to reduced soil fertility. In short, never apply lime until you have first manured the ground.

Lime helps to make potash and other minor elements in the soil available to the plants. It also affects the physical structure of clay soils by causing the tiny soil particles to join together and make larger crumbs, thus improving both aeration and drainage. It encourages worm activity, discourages slugs and in general helps to keep the soil sweet.

The simplest means of finding out whether your garden needs more lime is to collect a small sample of soil in a test tube. Then add a little rain water and just a few drops of hydrochloric acid (Spirits of Salt). If the mixture starts effervescing there is sufficient lime present for normal requirements. (If you want a more precise indication you can buy a soil testing kit.)

If your garden does need lime apply it at least one month before manuring or some three months afterwards, but never at the same time. Never add it at the same time as other chemical fertilizers and for preference apply it some two to three weeks before them. It is good practice to apply any bulky organic manure in the autumn and leave any lime dressing until the following spring. The quantity you need depends on the condition of the soil, the kinds of plants you plan to grow, and the type of lime you use. However as a general rule you can apply hydrated lime or quicklime at a rate of 120 g per square metre (4 oz per square yard) and ground limestone at a rate of 180 g per square metre (6 oz per square yard).

In excess lime is harmful to a wide range of plants and to some, such as rhododendrons, it can be deadly. However the general run of plants either like this condition or at least tolerate it.

Warning signals

If your garden is really short of essential plant foods the following symptoms will help you diagnose the trouble:

Nitrogen deficiency	Plant growth is retarded. Leaves are unnaturally pale
Phosphate deficiency	Seeds are slow to germinate Growing plants are stunted, with poor root development
Potash deficiency	Leaves are scorched around the edges
Lime deficiency	The soil is well fortified yet growth is still generally poor

Get the balance right

Some people are still convinced that chemical fertilizers are bad for the soil and bad for the plants, but this is simply not correct. For instance, both manure and sulphate of ammonia give your plants nitrogen. Manure also provides other matter which is very necessary to the soil, but it would take an awful lot of manure to provide as much nitrogen as can be obtained from a single sack of sulphate of ammonia.

The successful gardener applies organic matter from time to time as the situation demands, and he supplements it with the appropriate concentrated fertilizer when his garden needs it.

Garden Construction

Paths, Patios, Parking Areas and Driveways

Where a new garden is being laid out the construction of hard surfaces or the repair of existing ones is a job that will have to be tackled. You may have decided to build a hard standing area for the car. The driveway may need reconstructing. A patio or an additional path may be part of your new layout.

Hard surfaces for paths and patios

Ready mixed concrete is easy to use and hard wearing, but it's a dull material and it lacks character. Use it as a base and then surface it with a material of a more natural appearance; or better still, use other building materials such as logs, bricks, cobbles, crazy paving, cold asphalt, granite setts, gravel, natural stone, reconstructed stone and tarmacadam. There are of course some fine pre-cast paving slabs available in a range of colours and a variety of shapes; circular and hexagonal paving stones look particularly well in the right setting. (See diagrams 10a–e and diagrams 11a and 11b.)

Where hard surfaces abut the walls of the house make certain that the finished surface will be a couple of bricks below the damp course. Furthermore always ensure that any surface slopes away from the house so that rain water drains towards the garden.

Laying a log path

Wood can make quite an attractive and hard-wearing paving material and if you already have logs lying in the garden all you will have to do is hire a power saw and buy some drums of wood preservative. Cut the logs into sections some 20 cm (8 in) in length and then soak them in the preservative. Excavate the path to a depth of some 30 cm (12 in). Ensure that the subsoil is well consolidated (firmed) by rolling it and then add 10 cm (4 in) of coarse gravel and roll this. As it is compressed add more gravel, and continue rolling until you end up with a consolidated layer 10 cm (4 in) thick.

Next dip the lower end of each log in some tar and stand it upright in position on the gravel foundation. Keep the larger sections to the outside of the path and place the smaller ones down the centre. Any which sit

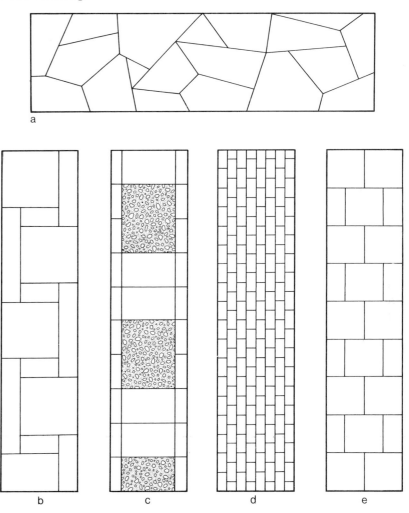

10 Five types of paving

a Crazy paving
b Creating a pattern with three sizes of
slab
c Using a combination of two sizes of
paving slab and sections set in pebbles
d Paving with old engineering bricks
e Paving with two sizes of slab

proud of the surface should be knocked home with a heavy hammer. The finished surface of the logs should be level with the surrounding ground.

The final operation is to spread a mixture of equal parts of sand and gravel over the surface of the path. This may need doing several times over the space of a week or two and on each occasion the material must be worked down between the logs with a yard brush. After a little while no further settlement will take place and you will have a very pleasant informal path for many years to come.

Brick and stone paths

There are various other possibilities to explore, such as making a brick path, or one of granite setts or cobbles. It all depends where you live and what is most cheaply and readily available. Start with a hardcore (broken bricks or rubble) or a gravel foundation. Next put down a layer of a dry mixture of sharp sand and cement in the proportion of 8 to 1, to a thickness of 2.5 cm (1 in). Bed the surfacing material on top of this.

Use a spirit level and levelling board to ensure that the surface is kept even. Various patterns can be created and materials can be intermixed to produce charming designs. Once you are satisfied with the design either damp the surface with a watering can to make the sand and cement mixture go hard, or wait for this to occur naturally. In either event keep off the surface until it has had a chance to harden properly. This may take anything from a few days to a fortnight, depending on weather conditions.

The 'stepping stone' path

Stepping stones in the lawn make a useful path for reaching a secluded corner of the garden (where the bonfire is made for instance) and ensure that the grass is not spoiled by traffic over its surface when it is wet. Set out suitably sized pieces of stone where the path is required, and then with the aid of a garden spade cut out the exact shape of each stone in the turf. Remove the turf and by the careful adjustment of the earth beneath set the stones in the ground with their upper surfaces level some 2 cm (3/4 in) below the level of the surrounding turf. Your mower cannot then be damaged by the stones.

The front path

For a path in regular daily use something more substantial is needed. Gravel paths are by far the cheapest to construct but they do need regular raking to remove ruts, and some hoeing or occasional spraying to destroy weeds. Paths in regular use should be at least 90 cm (3 ft) wide but if they are heavily used the width should be increased to anything from 112 cm (3 ft 8 in) to 145 cm (4 ft 9 in).

Set out pegs along the lines of the path and roughly level up the site with a spirit level and levelling board. On sloping sites see that the path slopes evenly. Excavate the site to a depth of 20 cm (8 in) and then consolidate it with a garden roller. When you are satisfied with the consolidation work introduce a layer of hardcore some 8 cm (3 in) in depth, using broken bricks, small stones, etc, and using the roller again consolidate this foundation layer.

When the hardcore is well firmed you can proceed with edging the path. Use Cuprinol-preserved wood with stout pegs driven into the ground at frequent intervals, or precast concrete or brick curbing pressed down firmly into a layer of wet concrete about 20 cm (8 in) wide along either side of the foundation layer. I prefer not to use wood as it is not so permanent and once it gives way it has to be replaced. The curbing must

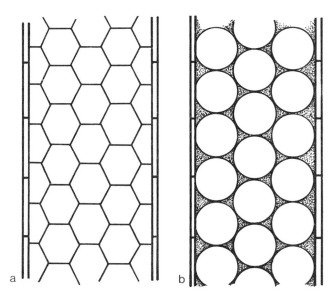

11 Hexagonal and circular pre-cast paving

a, b Two examples from a wide range of shapes and colours available to provide variety for paths and patios.

12 Haunching the curb

The curbing is pressed down into wet concrete and lined up; the concrete is then 'haunched up', *ie*, backed on the outer surface, using a builder's trowel.

1 Curbing
2 Hardcore foundation

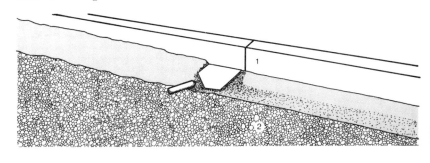

be laid so that its upper face will be finished flush with the surface of the path. The edge of the path should be kept down below the level of any adjacent lawn by at least 2 cm (3/4 in) to facilitate mowing.

Once the curbs have been adjusted to the correct lines and levels they should be haunched (or backed) on the outer surface with concrete (see diagram 12). A good mixture is 1 part cement, 2 parts sand and 3 parts coarse gravel. When the curbs have set hard, spread a layer of coarse gravel on the path some 6 cm ($2\frac{1}{2}$ in) in depth, and consolidate it with the roller. Finally put down a further layer of fine gravel and roll it in to a consolidated thickness which will bring it flush with the tops of the curbs. Once all this is completed restore the ground at the sides of the path so that no haunching is visible.

13 Laying a dry asphalt path

a Spread the asphalt over the gravel with a garden rake.
b Consolidate and repeat with a second layer, bringing the asphalt up to the level of the curbing.

Alternatively, for the second layer, after the first rolling, scatter coloured chippings and roll again.

1 Asphalt
2 Gravel foundation
3 Curbing

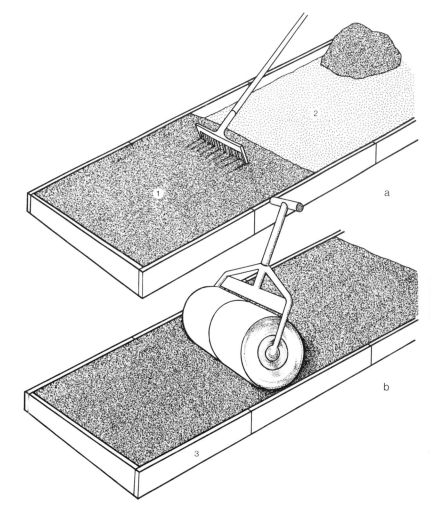

Laying a dry asphalt path

Near the house smooth hard surfaces should be provided. The easiest of these, an asphalt path, is really just one stage on from the gravel path described above. Once you have put down the coarse gravel and rolled it with the garden roller, add a layer of fine gravel to a consolidated thickness of about 3.5 cm (1½ in) and then 2.5 cm (1 in) of asphalt. Space the sacks of asphalt out by the side of the path so they can be reached easily and spread the contents over the gravel, levelling it off with the garden rake (see diagram 13a). It is best put down in two thin layers. Put down the first layer and when you are sure that it has been raked evenly roll it until it becomes firm. Repeat the procedure with the second layer, which should bring the asphalt flush with the top of the curbs. Handfuls of coloured stones can be scattered over the surface just before the final rolling so that they are then pressed down into the surface (13b).

Asphalt is reasonably durable and for cheapness ranks next to gravel.

Crazy paving and garden paving

If properly laid this ever-popular surfacing can create charming paths and patios. The preliminaries are as for a brick or stone path, excavating to the foundation level and then rolling the earth to consolidate before the introduction of the hardcore or coarse gravel, followed by fine gravel. Check the level of each layer before proceeding. With crazy paving and indeed all paving slabs used for surfacing it is necessary to include a layer of fine sharp sand some 2.5 cm (1 in) thick as a binding material over the foundations and this too must be well consolidated before laying the paving. The final stage is the application of some mortar to the under surface of each section of stone as it is set into position. The mixture is the 8 parts of sharp sand to 1 of cement previously recommended but for this purpose it is used in the wet state.

Crazy paving can vary in thickness so it is advisable to use a straight-edge and spirit level to see that the surface is kept smooth as shown in the drawing illustrating the laying of rectangular paving (see diagram 14a). Do not try to fill in all the small gaps as you go along but put down the larger pieces first and then come back later to fill up the gaps with the

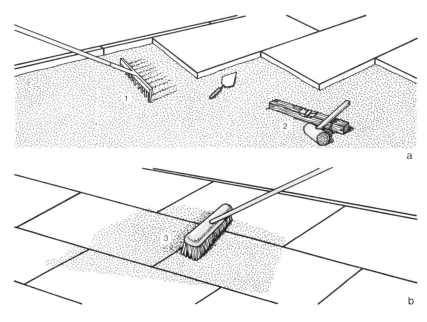

14 Final stages of laying garden paving

a Having laid the foundation as for brick or stone paths, lay a layer of fine sharp sand and consolidate. Apply mortar to the under surface of each section and set in position. With crazy paving especially it is essential to use a spirit level. Use a mallet and trowel to make adjustments.

b When paving is completed, brush sand over surface to fill joints.

1 Sand spread and rolled firm
2 Spirit level
3 Sand brushed into joints

smaller pieces. Filling the joints with coloured cement might be a further improvement. A mallet is useful for making minor adjustments to paving stones while they are being laid and final adjustments can be effected with a trowel. When the paving is completed brush fine sand over the entire surface to fill the joints (see diagram 14b).

When laying garden paving you can simply 'butter' the mortar on to the lower surface in the same way as for crazy paving, or you can put down a dry layer of mortar over the foundation and lay the paving into position as shown in the illustration of a paved path (see diagram 15). Some minor adjustments may be required but as the material is normally of uniform thickness this should not prove much of a problem. As long as you rely on the spirit level and the straight-edge rather than your eye this second method is probably the best.

15 The dry method of laying paving

1 Bedding layer of dry sand and cement mixture, 2.5 cm (1 in) thick
2 Coarse gravel, 5 cm (2 in) thick
3 Hardcore, 8 cm (3 in) thick
4 Curbing
5 Haunching of concrete
6 Paving slabs, 5 cm (2 in) thick, finished 2 cm (just under 1 in) below level of lawn

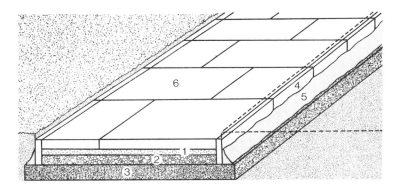

16 Constructing a concrete parking area or drive

1 Hardcore foundation
2 Wooden shuttering boards placed around boundary
3 Polythene sheeting or waterproof paper laid over hardcore
4 Concrete is laid in alternate sections, eg, b and d first, then, when these have set, a and c
5 Steel mesh reinforcement over first layer of concrete
6 Screeding board worked over surface to level it
7 Shuttering board forming expansion joint at intervals of 3 m (roughly 10 ft)
8 Second layer of concrete
9 Pegs

Parking areas and driveways

These areas have to carry a heavier load than paths and patios and the surfaces already described would break up under the weight because the foundations are not adequate. What you need is a substantial foundation layer of hardcore at least 15 cm (6 in) thick after consolidation. Use broken stone or broken bricks for this layer and then cover it with a 2 cm (3/4 in) layer of fine gravel. (See diagram 16.) At this stage place wooden shuttering boards into position around the boundary.

Next introduce about 15 cm (6 in) of ready-mixed concrete. The concrete should be put down in sections or bays divided by cross shuttering and should be spread in two layers with reinforcement wire mesh added before the second layer. Before starting to spread the

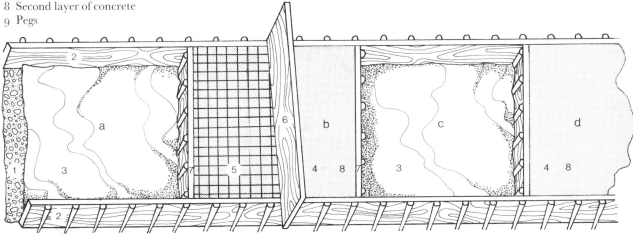

concrete lay sheets of waterproof paper or polythene sheeting over the foundation of hardcore. The actual lines and levels of the car park or drive will to a large extent be dictated by the general configuration of your site but when deciding about your formation levels give some thought to rain water dispersal.

Once the concrete has been laid use a screeding board across the shuttering boards to bring the surface level. When the concrete has hardened fill the other sections in the same manner but leave the cross shuttering in position to form the expansion joints which prevent the concrete cracking.

Once the concrete has had time to cure slowly it may be surfaced with any of the materials suggested in this chapter except logs. Bricks are liable to crumble, so if you do use them get only the hard red or blue engineering variety.

Dry Walls and Banks

If there are abrupt changes of level in your garden you will have to decide whether to face them with earth banks or with dry walls. When the change of level is part of the 'soft' landscape of lawn and earth it is preferable to create a bank and then turf it over. However, if the bank is very steep it will be difficult to mow, and it may dry out during hot weather, causing the grass to die. Steep banks should therefore be planted with ground cover plants.

If the change of level adjoins a patio or terrace the most satisfactory solution from a landscaping standpoint is to associate it with the hard surface by erecting a dry wall which will hold the earth firmly in position.

Building a dry wall
York stone is the most suitable material, though costly, but whatever type of stone you obtain it should be from 5 cm (2 in) to 20 cm (8 in) thick and of any size which can be reasonably handled. All the pieces should be reasonably flat so that they will fit together satisfactorily.

The area which will form the base of the wall should be fairly level and well consolidated. If the ground is loose and fluffy you will have to dig out a trench to produce a firm foundation, otherwise the wall will settle unevenly and very likely collapse sooner or later.

The stones should be laid in layers and bonded in exactly the same way as bricks in a wall: the stones in one layer are laid so that each is over the junction of two stones in the row immediately below. (See diagram 17a.) Spread a layer of soil as a fill some 3 cm (1½ in) thick over each row of stones and then bed the next row of stones on to this, planting as you go (see below). Ram the soil very carefully into the crevices where two stones meet, right through to the earth support bank at the rear (see diagrams 17b and 17c). There must be no air pockets otherwise plants growing in the wall will perish from lack of moisture. Sieving the soil makes the task of spreading and firming it much easier, and if it is a sandy soil mix it very thoroughly with granulated peat at the rate of 1 part peat to 3 parts soil, by bulk.

When you reach the top of the wall allow for a 15 cm (6 in) layer of well firmed soil as a capping layer. To preserve moisture place some large

17 Constructing single- and double-faced dry walls

a Stones laid in layers and bonded like bricks; soil spread between layers and rammed deep into crevices

b For a single-faced wall over 60 cm (2 ft) high extra long stones called tie-stones are laid at intervals endways on into the bank being supported

c For a double-faced free-standing wall the faces are inclined backwards at an angle of 1 in 6; the cavity is filled with earth which is rammed into position as walls are constructed

d Close-up of dry wall showing correct planting positions. Planting takes place at time of construction; plants are laid between joints with roots well spread out and on the layer of soil spread over the last row of stones

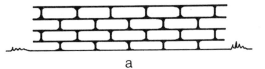

a

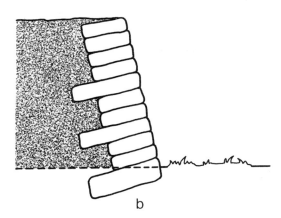

b

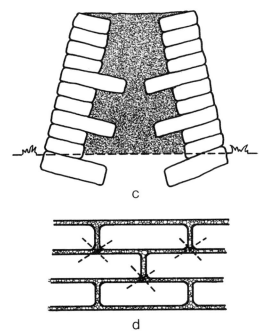

c

d

flat pieces of stone at appropriate intervals along the wall on top of this soil.

Except in the case of very low dry stone walls it is necessary to tilt the wall back slightly as you lay each row of stones. The ideal angle of the wall is 1 in 6. If you intend to build a wall much higher than 60 cm (2 ft) it is advisable to put in extra long stones as ties at intervals of about 2 m (6 ft 6 in) horizontally along the wall and every 40 cm (15 in) of its height. They are laid endways on into the bank and add considerably to the stability of the wall. (See diagrams 17b and 17c.)

Planting dry walls

Construction and planting of the wall is best undertaken during March and April when root growth is vigorous, and planting should take place as the wall is being built.

It will greatly help to establish the plants if you keep a bucket of puddly soil on hand and plunge the roots of each plant into this immediately before putting it into the wall. Spread the roots well out and set the plant at the bottom of a crevice between two abutting stones of the same layer, on top of the layer of soil which has been spread above the previous row of stones. This is the only position in the wall where plants will do well (see diagram 17d).

Once the wall has been created the easiest way of increasing the plant population is from seed. Mix the seed with just a little moist sand and press small amounts of the mixture into crevices in the wall. Cover these with small pieces of moss or moist peat to hold them firm.

Walls with two faces

You may plan to have a dry wall in your garden which stands by itself without a bank at one side. The general method of constructing it and planting it is just the same. (See diagram 17c.) However, the two faces have to be sufficiently far apart at the base to allow them to incline towards each other at an angle of about 1 in 6, and it is best to start with a space of 45 cm (18 in) between the inside edges. This space should be filled with well compacted soil, and will gradually become less as the walls gain height.

Pay attention to the lines and levels of the foundations and do not rush the job, for if the soil is not very well compacted the wall will buckle and in due course collapse. The top can be finished off with a narrow bed for planting, except in high rainfall areas where it is better to cap it with a coping stone. If the wall is to rise more than 60 cm (2 ft) do not forget to put in long stones endways on to give it extra stability and remember to allow more space between the inside edges of the base of the walls.

Plants for dry walls

The following list is only intended as a general indication of the types of plants to use in dry walls:

Achillea (yarrow)	*Helichrysum bellidioides* (everlasting)
Alyssum alpestre	*Hypericum fragile* (St John's wort)
A. saxatile	*Iberis sempervirens* (candytuft)
Aquilegia (columbine)	*Mesembryanthemum*
Arabis	*Nepeta faassenii*
Armeria maritima	*Polygonum affine* (knotweed)
Aubrieta	*Potentilla* (cinquefoil)
Campanula fragilis	*Saponaria caespitosa*
Cheiranthus (wallflower)	*Sedum*
Dianthus alpinus (pink)	*Sempervivum* (houseleek)
Erigeron mucronatus	*Silene* (campion)
Gypsophila prostrata	*Thymus*

If the wall runs east to west you should only plant shade tolerant species on the north side, such as

Acaena adscendens (New Zealand burr)	*Primula auricula*
Arenaria balearica	*Ramonda myconii*
Corydalis lutea	*Saxifraga*
Linaria alpina (toadflax)	

Spade Work

Now it's time to get down to the spade work: shaping your garden and preparing it for planting. By this time any repairs or construction of walls, paths and patios should have been completed, especially if you have had the work done by a contractor. Builders are notorious for the destruction they create, and it is a waste of time to start any work yourself until they have finished theirs.

What to leave untouched

Take a look at your landscape plan. Sites for such features as a shed, paddling pool, lily pond or greenhouse should not be dug over. Their foundations must be firm, and to this end the ground should have been undisturbed for many months, otherwise after the structure has been finished it could settle unevenly.

Topsoil is precious

The gardener is concerned with two distinct layers of earth, topsoil and subsoil, and it is very important to keep them separate. Topsoil is only 25–30 cm (10–12 in) deep – about the depth of a spade. This is the fertile layer, teeming with all those millions of infinitesimally small living organisms. Subsoil is comparatively lifeless, and during cultivation you must make sure that the topsoil does not get buried under the subsoil, otherwise it will become lifeless too.

Changing the level of the soil

Where there is room for earth shaping it helps to give the garden character. A perfectly level lawn like a billiard table is all right in a small area but a lawn with variations in level, yet having smooth running contours, is infinitely more attractive.

When raising the level of the soil you will need more earth, so clear a site for it near to where it is required. Next remove the topsoil from the area which is to be shaped and put it to one side, preferably on some sacking to keep it from getting mixed up with the soil on the ground. The area involved should then have successive layers of subsoil spread over it, each some 8 cm (3 in) deep, and these should be well consolidated layer by layer with a small hand roller or with your feet. Trampling the ground yourself is much slower but the mound will probably be subject to less subsequent settlement.

No matter how carefully you have consolidated the soil it will continue settling over the coming months, shrinking by anything from a quarter to a third. Consequently, if you want to get the size of your hillock as nearly correct as possible without having to add earth later, increase its total dimensions now by a quarter to a third and you will be about right. Then distribute the original topsoil evenly back on top.

If you fill hollows the filling should be left proud, but keep some spare topsoil to top-dress the surface as settlement goes on.

Existing trees and shrubs

If you plan to retain any trees or shrubs undisturbed you cannot simply heap soil around their stems and get away with it. There is a natural relationship between tree roots and the existing soil level, and if you vary this more than just slightly, within a year or two the tree may look distinctly sick and in another two years it will be dead. The same thing will happen if you try leaving a small gap around the stem by building a brick wall to keep the soil away from it. So if you keep existing trees or shrubs you will either have to replant them or, more simply, leave the ground around them at the old level.

Cultivating your site

Making a proper job of the garden means that someone is going to have to do all the spade work, and there are no short cuts. But at least it will only have to be done once. You won't be able to throw your spade away, but very little heavy work will be necessary once the new garden has been completed. In my view it is a mistake to keep on turning over the topsoil at frequent intervals. It doesn't happen in nature, and each time we do it we destroy a little of the humus.

When tackling a garden from scratch it is quite common to find that the ground is as hard as concrete. If it is really bad and is full of builders' debris, you may have to use a pick on the most difficult patches. It is no use getting a machine cultivator, for under such conditions the tines will break or throw large objects around. These machines are only useful on large open sites where the ground has been cultivated before.

You may need to turn the soil over only to a single spade's depth ('single spit digging') or to the depth of two spades ('double digging'). If the ground has been very compacted over the years the surface will have become extremely hard, and the subsoil will have developed a hard impervious upper layer. Double digging breaks up this layer and lets rain water drain away freely instead of forming pools on the surface. It also improves aeration, opens up the subsoil to soil organisms and plant roots, and enables the earth to warm up earlier each year.

Single spit digging

The cultivation of topsoil only is illustrated in diagrams 18a–f. The stages are as follows:

1 Put down a line along one edge of your piece of ground, and using this as a guide take out a trench to the depth of the spade and the width of the spade. Transfer the soil from this first trench to the other end of the plot, next to the line where you plan to dig your last trench (see diagram 18a).

2 With your garden line, mark out another strip of land one spade wide for your second trench. With the aid of the spade, shave any vegetation off the surface of this strip and put it in the bottom of your first trench.

18 Single spit digging

With this method, each trench is filled by the soil excavated from the succeeding trench except for the last, which is filled with soil taken from the first (see page 33).

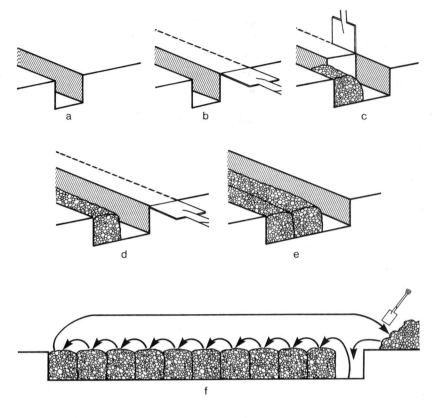

Perennial weeds should not be buried but tipped onto the rubbish heap. Any manure or other bulky organic matter which you plan to incorporate should now be spread in the bottom of the trench (see diagram 18b).

3 Begin the second trench by nicking the ground with your spade at right angles to the first trench, to break up the earth into manageable pieces. Plunge the spade into the ground parallel with the first trench, turning the spadefuls over and placing them neatly into the first trench in the same way that tiles lie on the roof of a building. Take care to keep this trench to a full spade's depth, but never try to take too big an amount of soil on the spade at once. It is far better to go up and down the strip two or even three times (see diagram 18c).

4 Mark the next strip and proceed with steps 2 and 3 as above (see diagram 18d).

5 The second trench is now filled with soil and the third trench has been created (see diagram 18e).

6 Go on in the same way until you have dug up the last trench, then fill it with the soil you originally removed from the first trench (see diagram 18f).

Double digging

In double digging (see diagrams 19a–g), twice the depth of soil is disturbed and turned over, but you *must* keep the second or subsoil spit of soil at the lower level and fill the first spit with topsoil only.

1 Mark out a strip of soil the width of two spades, putting down a line at either side. Strip off the vegetation and move this to the other end of

the plot. Dig out the trench to one spade's depth, taking care to keep the spade vertical all the time, and remove the earth to the other end of the plot where the last trench will be filled (see diagram 19a).

2 Stand in the bottom of the first trench and dig it over lengthways to a further spade's depth, taking care to break up the soil with the blade of the spade as the work proceeds (see diagram 19b).

3 Move your line two spades' widths further on. Then strip any vegetation which may be present and put it into the first trench, which you have just finished digging over. Add any manure or other organic matter required (see diagram 19c).

4 Dig over the newly stripped area and transfer the topsoil to the first trench (see diagram 19d).

5 Stand in the bottom of the second trench and scrape out any loose soil which may remain and place this on top of the soil which has just been moved to fill the first trench. Now dig over the second trench to a second spade's depth (see diagram 19e).

6 Repeat the same sequence from step 3 to step 5 until the whole of your plot has been double dug (see diagram 19f).

7 Fill the last trench with the topsoil you removed from the first trench (see diagram 19g).

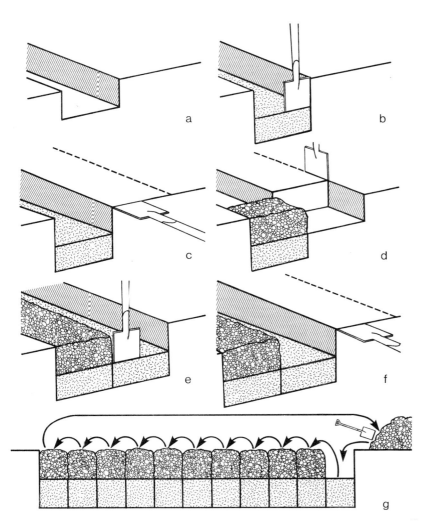

a

b

c

d

e

f

g

19 Double digging

Each trench is twice the width of the spade and after a spade's depth of topsoil has been transferred to preceding trench the subsoil is dug to a spade's depth (see page 34).

Importing new soil
By the time your work is completed there may be a shortage of soil, particularly if you have had to remove quantities of stone and bricks or if you have undertaken a lot of earth shaping. This means that some soil will have to be brought in, and you must be very careful where you get it from. It is surprising what poor varieties of soil many contractors will try to pass off as good loam.

Visit the site where the new soil is to come from and make sure that it is of good quality. If it contains a lot of stones and rubbish you will be no better off for having it. If it is topsoil but has been stacked in a heap for more than six months it will have lost most of its fertility.

If you only want the odd lorry load of topsoil and you are getting it from a large site where there are lots of earth works in progress, it would pay you to hire your own vehicle and collect your own soil. Alternatively, visit the site, get speaking to one of the drivers, and offer him a suitable tip on top of the contractor's price. With a bit of luck he will see that any stacked soil you have delivered is only from the top 30 cm (12 in) of any heap which you have inspected and agreed to accept.

The abrupt change of level in this garden would make it difficult to mow if it were completely turfed over. Instead the steep slope has been built up with low walls to achieve an attractive terraced effect (see page 29).

Above: front basement areas are a common feature of Georgian and Victorian town houses. Maximum use has been made of this limited space by the inclusion of a window box and a variety of free-standing plant containers.

Right: even if you have no garden at the back of your house or flat, a little imagination and effort can suggest opportunities for the cultivation of plants at the entrance. Here a combination of hanging baskets, window boxes (78–82) and plant containers of varying shapes and heights provides a welcoming display.

First
Impressions

The front entrance to your house is all-important. What can be more satisfying than to come home after a hard day's work and be greeted by a beautiful display of sweet smelling flowers and foliage? And first impressions count with your visitors too.

You need to consider what is the most appropriate arrangement of plants for your particular entrance. Diagrams 20 and 21 demonstrate what can be done with two very different types of house.

Whatever arrangement you decide to have, avoid introducing anything which will affect the functional purpose of the entrance, such as creepers which drip rain-water down on the head of anyone standing on the doorstep. And take care not to overdo it; large displays are not necessary or desirable. What is needed is something relatively simple which provides a splash of colour with either its foliage or its flowers.

Canopied entrances

If you have a canopy you can grow some form of climber around the doorway (see pages 94–97). Some canopies have timber supports which in turn are held in position by short stone or brick walls. If yours is of this type then you could contemplate incorporating two window boxes, one to fit neatly upon the top of the wall at either side of the door, between the wall of the house and the timber support.

If there is a canopy without any visible means of support, consider introducing a hanging basket, suspended at one side of the door or the other. It may be feasible to have two baskets, one at either side. (Hanging baskets are described in detail on pages 80–82.)

If there isn't a canopy, consider the possibility of adding one, because they are not only handy when you are fumbling for the door key in a downpour but they also extend the range of possibilities for the gardener. There are a number of designs available which are quite lightweight yet sturdy, and any reasonably handy do-it-yourself person could soon fix one into position. Most of them are capable of carrying at least one hanging basket. However, if you don't own your house you had better find out what the landlord's reaction will be. If you do own the property you would be well advised to enquire whether you need planning permission to install a canopy.

Unrelieved brick or stone walls are common in towns and cities and can be very depressing. A few climbers, either self-clinging or trained against supports, can transform them and soften the harshest of surfaces.

Other methods of display

If you can't have a canopy there are several other possibilities. Is there a window sill at one side of the door, or both sides? Window boxes should be easy to install (see pages 77–80).

What about a raised bed to one side of the entrance? The soil can be held in position by a low brick or stone wall. Even the idea of building a dry wall (see page 29) is worthy of consideration. Make a point of locating the damp course and ensure that the soil level comes no higher than two bricks below it.

What about standing a long teak trough against the wall? It might also be possible to fix brackets for a whole row of hanging baskets along the wall, either all in a straight line or staggered at different levels near the door. Metal brackets can support pots of cascading plants.

If there are steps leading up to the entrance see if there is room for tubs of conifers or flowering shrubs at either side. A fashion recently revived is to have bay trees growing in tubs at both sides of the front door of large town houses. Neatly trimmed to shape these shrubs look extremely attractive and indeed have become something of a status symbol.

Where the entrance is set back within the building line, climbers on the outer wall are a possibility.

If a porch faces north the range of plants is more limited, but this can be overcome to some extent if artificial strip lighting is available on dull days. Many plants will grow quite well with only about a third of the sunlight they receive on one of our brightest summer days. (See pages 79–80.)

Choosing containers to match the entrance

Consider selecting an oak container because your door is of grained oak, or a stone or marble one which will match the surface upon which it stands. If the door is painted you could paint some bowls or tubs the same shade. Or if there is decorative metalwork at the entrance then by all means choose metal stands for your containers.

As a general rule avoid loud colours, and if painting your own receptacles use pastel shades, for it is the foliage and flowers which are to be the centre of attraction. The receptacles should marry into their surroundings harmoniously, and if they do this and are the correct size and type for the plants then all will be well and the scheme will work perfectly.

Arrangements for an enclosed porch

An enclosed porch is likely to have glass in its roof, sides or outer door. If it is also large enough and receives some sun each day, it is a bit like a small greenhouse. You can plan for more tender ornamental plants and if you provide some winter warmth from a tubular electric wall heater the range can be almost infinite.

You could try *Acalypha hispida* with its long red tassles of flowers. *Anthurium scherzerianum* (flamingo flower) can be made to flower profusely throughout the year. Both red and orange varieties look exceedingly attractive with their evergreen foliage. *Begonia* 'Gloire de Lorraine' is a very useful winter plant and of course the summer flowering tuberous-rooted begonias do much better when given protection from the wind and rain. It is perfectly possible to grow *Bougainvillea* in a porch with a glass roof but if it is in full sun all day it should be given some shade by keeping it on the eastern side. *Begonia rex* can provide a fine display if

given just a little shade, but if you want a really outstandingly colourful pot plant grow *Caladium bicolor*.

If there is room you could have one or perhaps two hanging baskets inside the porch. Of course you must remember that this is the entrance to your home, not a greenhouse, so use controlled moderation in your choice of material.

The front garden

First take stock of your front garden, its size and shape in particular. Ask yourself these questions:

Is it paved, or partly paved?
Are there any shrubs or other plants growing in it which are worth
  saving?
Are there any fences, hedges or walls between your house and those
  of your neighbours?
What about the view from the houses opposite?
Is the garden in a sunny or shady position?

Before you decide what to plant, note what seems to grow best in your neighbours' gardens. Take a careful look at the soil and find out what needs to be done.

Generally speaking front gardens are not designed for sitting in, but some are so situated that they can be developed along the lines described for the back garden (see pages 112–114). Many, however, are so tiny and

20 Informal treatment for a Victorian frontage
1 *Parthenocissus henryana*
2 Summer bedding plants in flower boxes
3 Rectangular container holding bedding plants nestles in a corner
4 An arrangement of hexagonal pre-cast concrete plant containers of varying heights; the containers are composed of a number of segments so that the heights can be adjusted to create a composite design
5 *Thuya plicata* 'Zebrina'
6 Car parking space

21 A suitable display for a period town house of confined frontage – colourful, but not overdone

1 Large concrete containers permanently planted with conifers
2 Framing the conifers, bedding plants in summer followed by flowering bulbs in spring
3 Hanging baskets

open that one's range is limited. First decide whether you want an uncluttered view from your windows or whether you would prefer some privacy. A few shrubs might provide all the seclusion you need, but if there is not sufficient room to plant them you will have to grow some climbing plants up a fence (see pages 94–97). This method of screening takes up very little ground space, yet once established it can be every bit as effective as a hedge.

Where only a small strip of earth is available it might be best to pave it over and put down plant containers. Or perhaps you could plant one or more beds of roses (see pages 83–89).

Where the front garden is of less modest proportions you could consider creating a lawn with a small border of flowers. Vast displays of annual bedding are not necessary. The flowers can be interspersed with dwarf evergreen shrubs for extra effect. If you decide in favour of paving you can still leave a border for bedding plants and shrubs. One or two ornaments or small statues can do much to add to the interest of a paved surface but they must be carefully chosen and of good quality.

If there is no real boundary between your house and that of your neighbours, *Buddleia alternifolia* makes a very useful informal hedge. If you fancy something a bit thorny to keep out children and dogs, *Berberis aggregata* grows into a fine impenetrable hedge. *B. verruculosa* is slower growing but can in time reach a height of 1.5–2 m (5–6½ ft). For more information about hedges and screens, see pages 90–93.

Dwarf conifers can play a useful part in your layout. *Juniperus communis hibernica* (Irish juniper) forms a compact and slender column of glaucous silver, height about 3 m (10 ft). *Juniperus procumbens* (creeping juniper) has the same coloration but grows no more than 30 cm (12 in) high, while spreading out to cover an area of up to 4 square metres (roughly 4 square yards), forming excellent ground cover for a sunny situation. *Picea pungens prostrata* (blue spruce) is silver-green, ground hugging, slow growing. The cypress *Chamaecyparis lawsoniana* 'Winston Churchill' forms a dense broad column of a rich golden yellow. There is a wide range of differently shaped conifers from silvery green to yellow and then on into blue-green. Visit your local garden centre to see which are available, as they are particularly useful for winter decoration of the front garden.

Treatment for a front balcony

If you have a large balcony over the front entrance it could be just the spot to develop as a roof garden. (See pages 115–118.) If there is only a narrow balcony with a wrought iron railing it might be better simply to arrange several balcony boxes behind the railing.

Lush Lawns

When constructing a new lawn should you use turf or sow grass seed? There is no simple answer to this question, for both methods have advantages and disadvantages. Whichever method you adopt, however, the site should have been well dug over some months earlier and have had time to settle. The soil should have been well firmed and raked (see diagrams 22a and 22b), free from minor hollows and humps. It need not be perfectly level; indeed smooth running contours are much more attractive, and all you need is a shape that the mower can traverse without scalping the ground.

Turfing

Turfing is certainly the quickest method but it is also the most expensive. However, the lawn is ready for use in a matter of weeks and, if carefully watered in dry spells, it should suffer no setbacks. The main difficulty is to locate good quality turf and the next is to get it laid quickly before it deteriorates, for the best time for lifting and laying turf is when the weather is least reliable.

The turf should be delivered cut into sections 30 cm by 100 cm (1 ft by 3 ft) and 4 cm ($1\frac{1}{2}$ in) thick (see diagram 22c). Start turfing from one corner of the site, laying the turves like bricks in a wall (see diagram 22d). As the work proceeds put down planks over the turf to avoid making depressions with your feet. If all the turves are of the same thickness you only need to adjust the soil beneath them as may be necessary to produce a smooth surface (see diagram 22e).

Once the turf has been laid, dust a mixture of equal parts of peat and sand over the lawn and then brush it into the joints between the turves. Never roll the grass until the roots have had time to take hold, and even then give it only a light rolling. This should then be followed by a further dressing of peat and sand, which is again brushed into the joints. Turfing is best undertaken in the autumn and winter but may be done at other times providing you water the grass copiously.

A new lawn from seed

Sowing grass seed is certainly the cheapest way of producing a lawn but it will be some eighteen months before you get good fibrous turf, and this is the main disadvantage of this method. You can sow a new lawn in spring, but early autumn is the best time, for it gives you the whole summer to prepare the ground. The soil is warm at this time and the air is humid, and these are ideal conditions for rapid seed germination. Spring sown seed is slower to establish itself and if the summer is dry the new grass can have a difficult time. Some patches may fail completely and need re-seeding later, and artificial watering washes ungerminated seed about, causing more bare patches. The birds cause problems too.

When preparing the site do not add bulky organic matter. This will only encourage soft rank growth during the winter, making the young grass highly susceptible to frost damage and fungi diseases. If the soil is heavy incorporate coarse sand, peat, or power station ash if available, forking it in lightly to a depth of 10 cm (4 in).

Creating a good seedbed is crucial to producing a good lawn. Go over the site with your feet and firm every square centimetre of it, a little at a time, using a rake to draw soil into hollows and reduce pronounced humps. A roller will not produce such good results as this slower method, and as the lawn is going to be with you for many years it is worth the extra trouble. The aim is to produce a fine dust-like tilth some 2 cm (3/4 in) deep, with a firm base beneath in which the germinating seed may anchor its roots. During the summer work the hoe and rake over the site from time to time to kill any weeds.

The very finest lawns are those produced from seed, for then you can choose the specific quality you need. This is rarely the case with lawns created from imported turf. Indeed, to establish the very finest of ornamental lawns you need only a simple blend of two grasses:

> 80% Chewings Fescue
> 20% Browntop Bent

Another slightly coarser but still quite good mixture is:

> 55% Chewings Fescue
> 35% Crested Dog's-tail
> 10% Browntop Bent

If you want a mixture that will stand up to children's games fairly well then consider:

> 30% Perennial Rye-grass, S23
> 30% Perennial Rye-grass (New Zealand)
> 30% Creeping Red Fescue
> 10% Browntop Bent

Sowing

To encourage rapid establishment of the grass you can dress the seedbed with Growmore fertilizer, at the rate of 60 g per square metre (2 oz per square yard). Do this several days before sowing and rake the fertilizer into the surface.

Grass seed is sown at the rate of 60 g per square metre (2 oz per square yard). To ensure even distribution you should divide the seed into two equal amounts and then sow it by hand, walking up and down the garden scattering the first half and then back and forth across it with the second half. Throw it about with confidence, for this is the only way to avoid missing the odd place. However, choose a day with little wind otherwise most of the seed may be blown into other gardens. Don't worry if some of the seed strays a little beyond the lawn area. When the grass has formed turf, use a line and spade to trim it back to the right place.

Rake the seed into the surface immediately so that little is visible to the

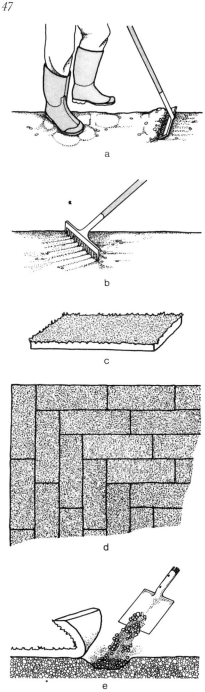

22 Constructing a new lawn with turf

a Firm the ground by treading and take excess soil from humps to fill hollows

b Rake again to create a good crumb structure on the surface

c Turves cut in sections 30 cm (1 ft) by 1 m (roughly a yard) by 4 cm (1½ in) thick

d The turves should be bonded like bricks with no two joints opposite each other

e As turfing proceeds, make minor adjustments to the soil bed

birds. Never roll the seedbed after sowing; this will only cause slower germination. Only roll the grass when it is some 10 cm (4 in) high and in need of cutting for the first time, so that the mower will not pull it out of the ground. If you can, employ a side-wheel mower for the first cut.

Mowing the grass

Mowing doesn't simply keep down the grass; it also improves its vigour and quality. Frequent mowing encourages the growth of the finer grasses and discourages the coarser ones, which in time will become less dominant.

Ideally you should adjust your mower to cut at a height of 2 cm (3/4 in) for this leaves the grass long enough to look attractive without starving the roots or scalping the surface. In shady areas the grass should be allowed to grow longer and the height of the cut should never be less than 6 cm (2½ in). Collect cuttings in the grass box; don't leave them on the ground for it will cause the lawn to become thin and patchy in time. And never put mown grass into the compost heap directly after applying selective weed-killer to your lawn. The weed-killer may affect the plants you fertilize with the compost.

When buying a mower, choose the model which is least fatiguing to handle; weight has nothing to do with its effectiveness. For a small town garden it should have a cutting width of 30–50 cm (12–20 in).

Never cut the grass by shunting backwards and forwards. The right way is to move forwards in one continuous motion at a steady pace. With hand-propelled machines regular mowing every 7 to 10 days will greatly reduce the effort involved, for long grass chokes the machine. Never cut in the same direction each time, for this only makes the grass lie away from the cutting cylinder and creates a washboard effect. If you like 'zebra stripes' first mow round the perimeter twice and then backwards and forwards in parallel lines from side to side. Make sure that each line just meets up with the preceding one. Never mow under wet conditions, for this can ruin the structure of the soil and cause drainage problems. Mow occasionally during winter, when there is no frost, to keep your lawn neat and tidy.

Maintaining a healthy lawn

Diagrams 23a–e illustrate how to keep your lawn healthy. You should take the following steps:

1 In both spring and autumn rake your lawn to remove matted dead grass (see diagram 23a).
2 In autumn spike the lawn to a depth of 10 cm (4 in) at 10 cm (4 in) intervals (see diagram 23b).
3 In spring apply a complete lawn fertilizer at 60 g per square metre (2 oz per square yard) and work this well down by light sweeping movements with a besom broom or a piece of old rough matting (see diagram 23c).
4 Keep the grass down to a height of 2 cm (3/4 in).
5 Keep rolling to a minimum. Once in spring and again in autumn is quite enough (see diagram 23d).
6 Lime is bad for your lawn because it causes worm and weed problems and makes the finer grasses die out. Apply it only rarely, for instance when the grass is very sparse and contains a great deal of moss. Even then do not lime without the advice of a turf expert.

23 Maintaining an established lawn

a Rake through in spring and autumn to remove dead growth and encourage new growth

b In the autumn spike the lawn to a depth of 10 cm (4 in) at 10 cm (4 in) intervals; this aerates soil, improves drainage and stimulates root activity

c Work a spring fertilizer down into the lawn with a besom broom to stimulate the grass

d Use the roller once only in spring and once only in autumn

e Apply a selective weed-killer during May and June from a watering can, using a wide boom attachment to spread the weed-killer

7 Eradicate worm casts with Chlordane Wormkiller.

8 Control weeds with selective weedkillers containing MCPA and 24D formulations. Apply them during May and June (see diagram 23e).

9 Moss is readily killed by either liquid or powder moss-killer.

10 The repair of worn patches by re-seeding is best carried out in early autumn and with new turf during autumn and winter. Diagrams 24a and b demonstrate how to repair worn edges.

24 Repairing the lawn edges when there is no spare turf

a 1 Cutting along a garden line behind the damaged edge
  2 Damaged turf edging
  3 Path curbing
  4 Cutting the worn-edged turf into pieces

b 5 The pieces have been lifted and reversed
  6 A good new edge has been created
  7 The gap between the turf is filled with sieved soil, firmed by treading, raked, and sown with grass seed which is worked into soil with the rake

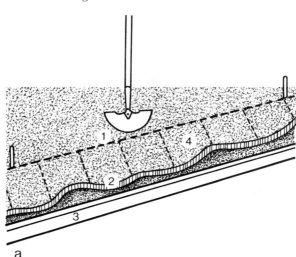

a

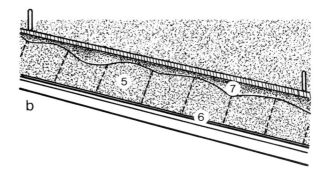

b

Grass substitutes

You can have a green sward in your garden without growing grass. Two possibilities are worthy of serious consideration:

Anthemis nobilis (chamomile) is a herb which produces low, dense growth and has been used since the 16th century for drought-resistant, aromatic lawns. The aroma is most noticeable when the plants are slightly crushed under foot. Raise young plants from seed sown in seed trays. Prepare the ground as if you were going to turf it (see page 46), then set out the plants 15 cm (6 in) apart in each direction during April or May. Allow them to flower the first year, as this encourages them to spread and form a dense carpet. During the second and subsequent years cut the lawn with the blade of the mower set at 4 cm ($1\frac{1}{2}$ in) or higher. Dress it with a good general fertilizer each spring.

Mentha pulegium (pennyroyal) is another herb which has an agreeable fragrance. It is best suited for lawns on moist ground and in partially shaded areas, but is of little value in districts with low annual rainfall or on sandy well-drained soils. You can sow seed during spring or spread the plant vegetatively by dividing the roots during the autumn. In dry spells it is necessary to keep the lawn watered. Some annual renovation will be found necessary on established lawns and this is best done by division of the roots of the existing plants. A spring dressing of a good general fertilizer is desirable.

Spring and Summer Bedding

Keeping your garden ablaze with colour calls for two separate plantings each year. Flowers for spring can be prepared the previous year, while you can grow summer flowers during the early months of the year you need them.

You can produce a wide array of flowers provided you have a cold frame or a few cloches. A greenhouse is useful but is not necessary for many of the summer plants, and in the case of the spring flowering kinds no protection whatever will be required.

Preparing the ground

Success depends on careful planning and preparation of the beds before planting begins, for there is not much time to spare between the removal of one lot of plants and their replacement with the next.

It is important to apply the correct fertilizers to your beds and borders when they are free of plants, to help the soil sustain the heavy demands upon it. Garden compost and farmyard manure are useful, but be careful. Adding too much in spring will result in the growth of foliage at the expense of flowers. Too much in autumn will almost certainly encourage slugs, which will busy themselves consuming not only the organic matter but also the bulbs you have planted for the spring display. To avoid these difficulties fortify your soil with only gradually available organic fertilizers such as fish meal or bone meal. Put it on after cultivation and prior to planting out the summer bedding, at the rate of 100 g per square metre (about 3 oz per square yard).

Bedding plants do not grow well without good root anchorage, so when the various stages of cultivation are completed tread the ground thoroughly to ensure that it is well firmed, and then rake the surface. Once you have planted out your bedding apply finely divided sedge peat to the surface. This will help to smother weeds and maintain soil moisture, while at the same time adding much needed humus to the soil. Peat can be applied twice a year if necessary. During the autumn it will be dug in and at the same time you can add a light dressing of manure, garden compost or shoddy (woollen waste). This is all that is necessary to maintain soil fertility and produce the best results.

Growing plants from seed

Growing your own plants from seed certainly adds considerably to your sense of satisfaction, and the chances are that you can find some space for doing so if you really want to. Have you a greenhouse? Can it be heated in any way from mid-January to mid-April? Have you a 'cold' frame? You may have several cloches, which will do just as well. If not you could buy some, or make some out of odd bits of material such as PVC sheeting, wire netting and plastic sheeting, or possibly wooden boxes and pieces of glass. You can even use a verandah as a greenhouse in winter.

Seeds which have to be sown early can go out into a cold frame, with a little extra protection on frosty nights from some pieces of old sacking held in place with lumps of stone or lengths of timber. If you haven't a cold frame, you could start seed trays inside clear plastic bags on the kitchen window sill. Otherwise you will have to content yourself with sowing hardy annuals and biennials, buying the more tender subjects from your local nurseryman. In any case, plan your needs in advance.

Buying seeds

When buying seeds, read the small print on the back of the packet. This will tell you whether the seeds have been treated in any way, and though treated seeds are more expensive they will give you a better success rate. A dressing of Thiram helps to protect them against damping-off. This disease causes the collapse of the seedling stem just above ground level; *Antirrhinum* and *Lobelia* are perhaps the most vulnerable to attack. Tiny seeds are very difficult to handle, and seedsmen make them larger by giving them a thick coating. These are called 'pelleted' seeds and can be easily spaced out, thus avoiding wastage. The coating crumbles away almost at once when it comes into contact with moist soil.

Some firms market carpets of seeds which you simply put on the ground and cover with a little soil. You can even obtain small plastic seed trays filled with compost and ready sown.

In recent years seedsmen have concentrated on artificial cross-pollination and have succeeded in producing hybrid varieties of superior quality called 'F_1 hybrids' because they are the first child of the marriage. They usually flower earlier and their flowering period is longer. The flowers are superior and of greater uniformity. These advantages are not fixed permanently and the seedsmen have to cross-pollinate the parent varieties every time, so the method greatly puts up the cost of the seeds. Nevertheless the chances are that when you have once tried F_1 hybrids you will want to buy more.

Sowing and growing on

When sowing seeds you can use either the familiar John Innes Seed Compost or one of the modern soil-less composts. Press the compost moderately firmly into the seed tray, paying particular attention to the corners of the tray and ensuring that the finished surface is perfectly level. It must be uniformly moist at the time of sowing without being over-wet, so water the trays several hours before sowing and for preference the previous evening.

Sow the seed as evenly as possible over the surface. Some seeds have to be given a further light covering with compost while others germinate quite happily when simply given some darkness with a covering of glass or plastic plus thick paper. Wipe the moisture from the lower surface of the covering each morning and give the seedlings full light by removing the paper immediately you see the seedlings thrusting themselves above the compost. Depending upon the seeds and the temperature this may take only a day or two, or several weeks or even months. However none of the plants I suggest in the list below will keep you in suspense for very long.

Once the seedlings are large enough to be picked up by their seed leaves the time has arrived to prick them out into other seed trays. Most seedlings are pricked out individually some 5 cm (2 in) apart in each direction. Some can be put directly into the open ground where they are to flower, but in their early stages most plants require the protection of a garden frame or cloche. These should subsequently be hardened off before finally being planted out in the open during late May or early June according to local climatic conditions.

Buying seedlings

The alternative to sowing your own plants is of course to buy seedlings from a nursery, and this can be particularly worthwhile if you want the expensive F_1 hybrids. Some nurseries (e.g., Colegraves of West Adderbury, Banbury, and Oaker Nurseries, Yeldham, Halstead, Essex) produce trays holding a specified number of seedlings, which have to be ordered well in advance.

Designing the beds

When deciding which plants you are going to use, take into account the shape of the beds and both the height of the flowers and their colour in relation to each other. To know what quantities to buy you will have to consider the distance needed between the seedlings when they are finally planted out. As far as possible begin planting around the outside of the bed and work inwards. When sowing seeds or planting out seedlings you can mark the ground in a grid with a narrow piece of wood (see diagrams 25a and 25b). The method of sowing seeds in drills is illustrated in diagrams 26a–d, and the best ways of preparing holes for seedlings are illustrated in diagrams 27a and 27b.

Plants for a spring display

Alyssum saxatile compactum A hardy perennial produced either from seed or from cuttings secured in early June from firm young shoots. Insert in sandy soil under a cold frame and give some shade until rooted, then grown on without protection until required for permanent planting out. If growing from seed start in late March under a cloche or frame, or sow in late April in the open in very shallow drills and transplant into a small nursery bed some 10 cm (4 in) apart. It takes about two years

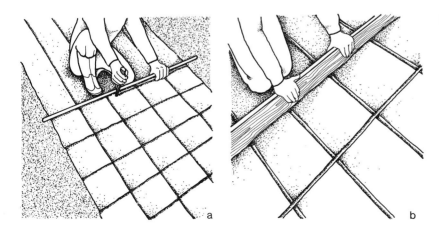

a

b

25 Marking the flower bed in a grid before planting seedlings

a Using a narrow piece of wood and a stake; the crossing points of the lines indicate the position for each plant

b Alternatively, the cross markings can be made simply with a piece of wood. This type of marking out can be adjusted to give the required planting distance

26 Preparing the seed drills

1 Rake the bed to create a fine, dust-like tilth (see diagram 26a)
2 Using a garden line and a broom handle, draw out a drill 1.5 cm (about ½ in) deep—the ideal depth to produce a good germination rate (see diagram 26b)
3 Alternatively, make the drill simply by pressing a stout bamboo cane into the soil surface; no line is needed (see diagram 26c)
4 After sowing the seed, cover it by drawing the back of a garden rake lightly along the seed drill (see diagram 26d)

Never use a hoe to draw out your seed drills—they will be far too deep and many seeds will die before reaching the surface

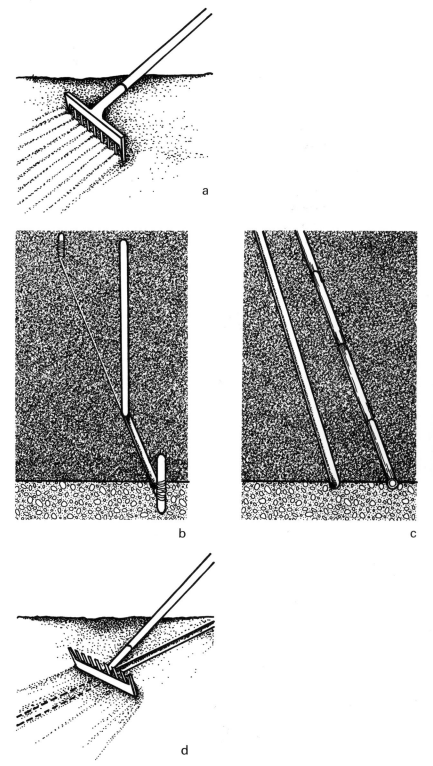

a

b

c

d

before really well established carpeting plants can be produced from seed, but as a permanent feature they are well worth growing. If producing from seed 'Golden Ball', with clusters of brilliant yellow flowers, is one of the most suitable for both rockeries and for spring bedding, growing only 20 cm (8 in) high. 'Silver Queen' grows to the same height and has pale lemon yellow flowers.

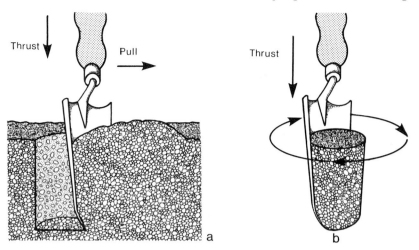

27 Preparing a planting hole

a If the soil is reasonably well drained, simply thrust the trowel into the soil and then draw it towards you

b With heavy, wet soil, thrust the trowel directly into the soil and twist it round full circle so as to remove a plug of soil

Bellis perennis (double daisy) An indispensable part of the spring display. It is dwarf, grows some 15 cm (6 in) high and produces an abundance of fully double daisy-like flowers from white through pink to various shades of red. Can be used for edging or bedding. As a carpet for spring flowering tulips it can produce some quite spectacular results. Sow in open ground about mid-May in very shallow drills and transplant into a nursery bed 10 cm (4 in) apart until a suitable size for bedding out in final positions during autumn. Spray aphis immediately with systemic insecticide when necessary to prevent characteristic stunted growth and distorted leaves. Can be propagated by division of roots after flowering. May flower both in spring and autumn if left undisturbed.

Cheiranthus cheiri (wallflower) One of the most popular spring bedding plants, with a delightful fragrance and wonderful range of colours. Wallflowers also make excellent carpeting for tulips, providing you choose the right colour combinations. Sow in shallow drills during late May/early June and transplant into a nursery bed 15 cm (6 in) apart until planted out into final flowering positions in autumn. Or sow pelleted seeds 3 weeks later, spacing them out in the drill and thus avoiding transplanting until the plants are due to be put in their final positions. The two methods produce plants of the same size at the same time. Pinch out the tips in early August to make them more bushy. On sandy soil work in a dressing of peat before sowing. In dry weather give the seedbed a good watering the day before sowing, and once the seedlings appear give a regular but light spraying each evening. Recommended varieties: 'Cloth of Gold', golden yellow large flowers; upright habit, 38 cm (15 in) high. 'Fire King', orange scarlet, compact habit, 38 cm (15 in). 'Ivory White', creamy white, 38 cm (15 in). 'Orange Bedder', rich orange shading apricot-yellow, dwarf compact habit, 30 cm (12 in). 'Scarlet Bedder', rich scarlet, very dwarf and compact, 20 cm (8 in). 'Vulcan', dark crimson, 30 cm (12 in).

Myosotis alpestris (forget-me-not) The blue flowers make a wonderful spring display. Sow in shallow drills in late May and early June on open ground in a somewhat shady position. Transplant into a nursery bed 10 cm (4 in) apart and leave to grow into sizeable plants for final planting out in autumn. When surmounted by a tulip such as 'Princess Margaret Rose', which is yellow and attractively edged and flushed orange-red, the results are truly magnificent. Good varieties: 'Blue Ball', deep indigo,

15 cm (6 in). 'Erect Blue Spire', vivid blue, 30 cm (12 in). 'Royal Blue', deep intense blue, 25 cm (10 in). Also available in red and white.

Primula Polyanthus A hardy perennial which makes an excellent display when grown in beds on its own. Seeds are available in separate colours or mixed shades. Sow in shallow drills in open ground in late May; transplant into a nursery bed 10 cm (4 in) apart until final planting out in autumn. The Blackmore & Langdon's strain has an exceptionally good colour range and large flowers. Other good strains include Dickson, Brown & Tait's 'Spring Glow', 'Giant Bouquet' and 'Giant Colossea', and Suttons' 'Pacific Dwarf Jewel' with its range of rich colours.

Plants for a summer display

Ageratum mexicanum is particularly effective, flowering the whole summer through. Scatter seeds over the surface of the compost in seed trays during early March. They need warmth for good germination but seedlings may be grown on quite successfully under cold frames. The final flowering position should be a warm sunny one. *Ageratum* is a good edging plant either on its own or with others such as *Alyssum*, *Calceolaria* and *Tagetes*, or it can take a more major role intermixed with *Geranium*, *Salvia*, *etc.* Good varieties: 'Blue Blazer' F_1 hybrid, large clusters of deep blue flowers, compact habit, 10 cm (4 in). 'Blue Ball', dark blue clusters of flowers, 15 cm (6 in). 'Blue Mink', powder blue, 20 cm (8 in). 'North Sea', reddish purple flowers which mature deep violet, 10 cm (4 in). 'Summer Snow', F_1 hybrid, dwarf, pure white, 12 cm (5 in).

Alyssum maritimum Most suitable as an edging for the formal bedding display and for rockeries. Sow in seed trays March/early April. These can be started off in a cold frame quite successfully provided they are covered with glass and paper during germination, and covered with sacking each evening to keep out the cold. Prick out seedlings in clumps of about half a dozen. Good varieties: 'Little Dorrit', pure white, 10 cm (4 in). 'Minimum, Extra Select', pure white, but more compact and of more creeping habit. 'Royal Carpet', rich violet purple, creeping habit, 10 cm (4 in).

Amaranthus caudatus (love-lies-bleeding) This has long, pendulous, deep crimson spikes of a weeping habit and apart from its value for bedding it is much loved by the flower arranger. Seeds are usually sown several to a station where each plant is to grow, in early May, and seedlings are subsequently reduced to one at each spot. Particularly useful for the larger border of annuals or in the herbaceous border where it may grow to some 75–100 cm ($2\frac{1}{2}$–3 ft). For beautifully coloured foliage choose *Amaranthus tricolor* (Joseph's coat). 'Molten Fire' has deep copper crimson leaves with scarlet poinsettia-like heads. When the sun shines the display is brilliant, and it deserves the sunniest position in the whole garden. A half-hardy annual, it should be sown in a seed tray during March and not be planted out until all danger of frost has ceased. Height 45 cm (18 in).

Antirrhinum majus (snapdragon) Best sown late February/early March on the surface of the seed compost. It has a prolonged flowering season if you remove the old spikes as soon as the majority of the flowers have faded. Height about 45 cm (18 in). Standard varieties include: 'Black Prince', deep crimson flowers, very dark foliage. 'Dazzler', brilliant scarlet.

'Golden Eclipse', very deep rich yellow. 'Malmaison', beautiful silver pink flowers, dark foliage. 'White Freedom', pure white. If you fancy F_1 hybrids consider the 'Sprite' or 'Coronette' series, which are among the best and available in a wide colour range.

Begonia semperflorens This fibrous-rooted begonia is an important addition to the garden. Can be grown very easily from seed providing you hold it at a minimum night temperature of 16°C (60°F) and slightly higher temperatures by day. Sow January/early February in a heated greenhouse or buy seedlings or plants. The following varieties grow to an intermediate height of about 20 cm (8 in): 'Butterfly Red', a robust compact free-flowering plant, does well in sunny yet exposed situations. 'Indian Maid', bright scarlet flowers, bronze foliage. 'Loveliness', rose pink. 'Snowbank', glistening white flowers in great profusion, light green foliage. There are quite a number of F_1 hybrids and you could do no better than to try some of the 'Thousand Wonders' series, height about 16 cm ($6\frac{1}{2}$ in).

Calendula officinalis (pot marigold) Thrives in almost any situation and any soil so long as drainage is satisfactory. Height varies from about 25 cm (10 in) to 70 cm (2 ft 4 in) and the taller ones make ideal cut flowers. Sow in seed trays in mid-March and immediately place out in a frame, or scatter a few seeds where you want them to grow and simply cover them with a cloche. Suitable varieties include: 'Apricot Queen', bright yellow, 60 cm (2 ft), 'Dwarf Double Golden Gem' and 'Dwarf Double Orange Gem', 30 cm (12 in). 'Fiesta Gitana Mixed', 25 cm (10 in). 'Geisha Girl', glowing orange incurved chrysanthemum-type flowers, 60 cm (2 ft). 'Rays of Sunshine' flowers in a whole range of colours from creamy rose to deep orange with many shades in between. Height 60 cm (2 ft).

Callistephus chinensis (China aster) Pelleted seed is available. Sow late March/early April in a cold frame. Discourage aphids by spraying shortly after bedding out with a systemic insecticide. Available in a wide range of colours are: 'Ostrich Plume', 45 cm (18 in). 'Dwarf Queen', with an abundance of large double chrysanthemum-like flowers, ideal for carpet bedding and window boxes. 25 cm (10 in). 'Waldersee' with masses of small double flowers, early in showing colour. 25 cm (10 in).

Clarkia elegans This hardy annual can be sown where it is to flower in early April. Further sowings may be made in early May and again in June to ensure a fairly lengthy flowering period. Protective covering is not necessary but if available will hasten germination. A packet of 'Royal Bouquet Mixed' will provide the full colour range with large flowers on spikes 45 cm (17 in) high.

Godetia (summer azalea) hybrids Marvellously beautiful hardy annuals, ideal for any town garden. Choose the sunniest location and if possible use pelleted seeds. Sow in open ground during March where the display is desired, as the seedlings are not keen upon being transplanted. 'Choicest Monarch Mixed', height 30 cm (12 in) produces a wide range of colour; so too does 'Double Azalea-Flowered Mixed', height 35 cm (14 in).

Heliotropum (heliotrope) Its deep violet flowers make a useful contrast to the colours of other summer bedding material but its main charm is its heady aroma. Sow in early February. Germination is a bit erratic and warm conditions are essential, so grow in a warm greenhouse or purchase a few plants at bedding-out time. 'Marine' is an excellent variety, height 38 cm (15 in).

Iberis (candytuft) A fragrant hardy annual, built for survival regardless of soil or situation. Sow as thinly as possible in open ground in either autumn or spring and leave the rest to Mother Nature. This is another species which does not take kindly to being transplanted. 'Dwarf Compact Fairy Mixed' provides a glorious mixture of colours, height 20 cm (8 in). If you prefer single colours consult any good seed catalogue.

Impatiens (Busy Lizzie or balsam) An annual gaining fresh popularity as an important carpet bedding subject, mainly due to the new 'Imp' and 'Minette' strains. These superior modern introductions are not affected by variable weather and flower profusely in shade or sun, providing a dazzling display of colour right up to the first frost. Sow in seed trays in mild heat, in mid-March, and then move seedlings into a cold frame or cloche. When first planted out regular watering is essential until the plants have grown sufficiently to shade their own roots. They are rather slow in getting established but once the foliage spreads out will never look back.

Lathyrus odoratus (sweet pea) About the only plant which demands a really fertile soil. With the taller growing varieties it is essential to provide a deep root-run, double digging the site and introducing a generous dressing of well rotted garden compost. At the beginning of the growing season supplement this with light dressings of dried blood. The seeds may be space-sown in seed trays, 5 cm (2 in) apart in each direction, during February or March in a cold greenhouse or cold frame, or in the open ground where they are to flower. If sowing in the open, space the seeds 20 cm (8 in) apart each way and no thinning will be necessary. Tall-growing varieties require canes or twiggy sticks later. Dwarf varieties are best for flower borders and window boxes and need no support. Dwarf strains include: 'Bijou', available in an excellent range of colours, 35 cm (14 in). 'Little Sweetheart', a compact little plant, 20 cm (8 in) in height, wide range of colours. Flowering commences early and continues over a long period so is an ideal bedding subject. The following tall varieties produce a brilliant display and are all very conspicuously scented: 'Gigantic', pure white, densely frilled. 'Winston Churchill', brilliant crimson, nicely frilled. 'Princess Elizabeth', salmon pink on cream ground. 'Air Warden', orange-pink. 'Cream Gigantic', rich cream. 'Mabel Gower', bright blue. 'Silver Cascade', bluish lilac.

Lobelia Extremely popular as an edging plant and often planted in association with *Alyssum*. Sow during February; some heat is essential for germination. May later be grown on in a cold frame protected by sacking on cold nights. Seedlings are pricked out in clumps of half a dozen. Most popular varieties are: 'Cambridge Blue', pale blue. 'Crystal Palace', dark blue. 'Mrs Clibran' deep blue flowers with conspicuous white eyes. They all grow to 10 cm (4 in).

Mesembryanthemum criniflorum (ice plant) Needs a dry sunny position, where it will produce a most marvellous floral display in an extensive range of pastel shades. Good for rock gardens and carpet bedding, and flourishes in coastal and other windswept districts. Sow in early March with some warmth to get it started and grow on in a cold frame, covering with sacking on cold nights. Recommended: 'Magic Carpet Mixed', glistening large daisy-like flowers, height 12 cm (5 in).

Nemesia strumosa A Charming annual and easy to grow. Likes a warm sunny spot and is available in many different colours. Sow in mid-March and protect with a frame. 'Blue Gem', 'Fire King' and 'Orange Prince' all bloom abundantly, but as the plant is at its best when you mix the full colour range in one display, try 'Strumosa Hybrida Compacta Dwarf Gem Mixed'. All grow to 22 cm (9 in).

Pelargonium, zonal (bedding geranium) This tender perennial is very important for beds, borders, hanging baskets, tubs and window boxes. More generally propagated from cuttings, which are best taken during August. The resulting rooted plants are given greenhouse protection with suitable heat during frosty weather. Alternatively grow on indoors or buy fresh plants in May. Heights 45–60 cm (18–24 in). The many beautiful named varieties include: 'Caroline Schmidt', cerise flowers and bright silver foliage. 'Gustave Emich', deep scarlet, double flowered. 'Hermione', white double-flowered. 'King of Denmark', bright rose pink semi-double. 'Mrs Henry Cox', pale pink flowers and tricolor foliage, in great demand. 'Orangesonne', orange double-flowered. If producing from seed start in early January in a heated greenhouse at 24°C (75°F). Prick out into small peat pots or similar, maintaining temperatures of 21°C (70°F) by day and 17°C (62°F) minimum at night. Move the plants into larger pots as they develop, taking care not to disturb the root-ball. Tap the plant out of its existing container, place some compost in the base of the new one, and gently lower the root-ball into position, making sure that it is far enough below the rim of the pot for easy watering. Finally work in additional compost around the sides and firm into position with your thumbs. Most suitable for this early sowing are the F_1 hybrids 'Carefree Bright Pink', 'Carefree Deep Salmon' and 'Carefree Fickle'. The latter is a good bicolor with bright scarlet florets and a white centre. The F_1 hybrid 'Sprinter' has bright salmon red flowers and is more dwarf and compact than other suitable varieties.

Petunia A particularly useful half hardy annual which needs a warm sunny situation. The F_1 hybrids have virtually replaced older varieties. Sow in late February/early March on the surface of the compost in the seed tray, without covering. Germinates quickly at 18°C (65°F). Prick out seedlings as soon as they have formed one true leaf. When established in trays they may be grown on in a frame with extra protection on cold nights. The number of varieties make one's mind boggle, but here is my brief selection. Best for window boxes and tubs are the F_1 hybrid Grandifloras: 'Cloud Petunia' comes in blue, lavender blue, pink, deep pink, red, white; is also available as 'Cloud Mixed' 30 cm (12 in) high with individual flowers of 10 cm (4 in) which very quickly cascade over the side of their containers. Best for weather resistance are the F_1 hybrid Multifloras: 'Resisto Blue', 'Resisto Red', 'Resisto Rose Pink'. For hanging baskets go for the 'Cascade' F_1 hybrids in blue, pink, red, and white or as 'Mixed Cascade'.

Phlox drummondii 'Grandiflora Mixed' is very easy to cultivate and is one mass of bloom throughout the summer in a rich range of colours, height 30 cm (12 in). Nana Compacta 'Improved Cecil Mixed' also comes in a spectacular range of colours, height 15 cm (6 in). Both are very reliable anywhere in the country providing they are given fertile soil. Sow mid-March/early April and protect with a frame.

Tagetes (marigold) The F_1 hybrids flower early and continuously, and often take only 6 weeks to produce the first flowers. Sow in late April in seed trays on the surface of the compost, then place directly in a cold frame. Among the masses of varieties which I could recommend are: 'Crackerjack Mixed', orange, yellow and gold double-carnation blooms 9 cm ($3\frac{1}{2}$ in) across, height 75 cm ($2\frac{1}{2}$ ft); 'Lemon Drop', bright canary yellow, 23 cm (9 in) high; and 'Naughty Marietta', a dwarf single French marigold with rich golden yellow flowers blotched maroon, height 30 cm (12 in). Where space is limited and you need a marigold of compact habit choose the 'Ladies' series, height 30 cm (12 in).

Tagetes signata pumila A very popular dwarf member of the marigold family. Very easily raised from seed, it begins to flower some 6 to 8 weeks after sowing and remains smothered with flowers all summer long. Height 15 cm (6 in). Use as an edging plant on its own or with lobelias such as 'Crystal Palace' or 'Mrs Clibran'. Sow in early April protected by a cold frame, or in the open where it is to flower in early May. Sow very, very sparingly in very shallow drills and subsequently thin out the plants to 15 cm (6 in) apart. Try: 'Carina', deep orange. 'Golden Gem', golden orange. 'Lemon Gem', bright lemon yellow. 'Lulu', yellow. 'Paprika', bright red-edged gold flowers.

Bulbs for Beds and Borders

Spring-flowering bulbs are particularly useful to bring a splash of colour to the garden from about mid-March to late May. They make a fine display when planted on their own and an even better one when interplanted with such spring bedding as double daisies, forget-me-nots, polyanthus and of course wallflowers.

Bulbs will grow in a wide range of soils as long as they are well drained and free from weeds. The fertility of the ground does not matter because they have a store of food to carry them through to maturity. Bulbs only deteriorate if left in the ground and those used for bedding are best thrown away or placed in some side border to become naturalized there. The quality of the flowers depends on the size of the bulbs and you must remember that you only get what you pay for.

The most suitable bulbs for formal beds and borders are hyacinths and tulips, with daffodils, crocuses and irises planted in side borders, among the shrubs and trees or, in the case of daffodils and crocuses, possibly naturalized in the lawn.

How to plant bulbs

You can plant bulbs with a trowel but I prefer a large flat-ended dibber made out of an old spade shaft and some 30 cm (12 in) long (see diagram 28). This ensures that the bottom of each hole is flat, with no chance of a cavity being left below the bulb where water could gather, and it also ensures that the bulbs are planted at the correct depth.

Diagrams 29a and 29b give you some tips on the best approach to planting bulbs, and also what not to do (see diagram 30). Note that different species require different depths and spacing (see diagram 31) and if some are planted deeper than others of the same sort they will bloom later.

In the heavier clays it pays to introduce about $2\frac{1}{2}$ cm (1 in) of coarse sand into the holes before actually planting the bulbs, as this greatly assists drainage and does much to prevent the bulbs rotting.

Always start planting around the outside of the bed, never the centre. Lay the bulbs out on the bed where they are to be planted before you make any holes, for in this way you can avoid running short when it is too late. Don't try to create complicated designs using many different colours, for they will rarely look quite as you had hoped. It is far easier to produce this type of result by growing bulbs between carpeting plants such as wallflowers or forget-me-nots or other suitable spring bedding plants (see pages 53–56)

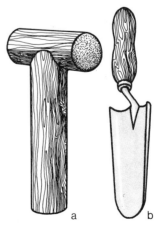

28 The tools
Flat-ended dibber made from old spade shaft (a), and trowel (b).

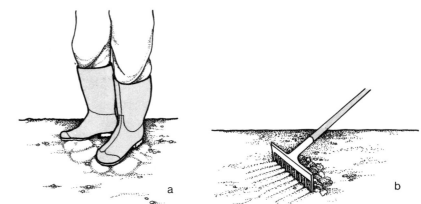

29 Planting bulbs
a Tread and firm soil before planting
b Rake bed before planting—and repeat
afterwards

Bulbs for formal bedding

Choosing suitable bulbs can prove quite daunting because there are so very many different types. Time of flowering also has to be taken into consideration, for some gardeners like a good display in April while others prefer May. Below I have set out what in my view are the best varieties for flowering from mid-March to May.

Informal planting

Here are some suggestions for bulbs that would look well beneath shrubs and trees, or on the rockery:

Allium Flowers June/July. Grows quite happily on all types of soil. Plant in autumn some 30 cm (12 in) apart and 8 cm (3 in) deep. *A. aflatunense*, large globular clusters of lilac-purple flowers, 75–90 cm (2½–3 ft). The cut flowers will last for several weeks. *A. moly* 'Luteum', bright yellow clusters of starry flowers, height 30–40 cm (12–16 in). *A. neapolitanum*, pure white flowers, about 45 cm (18 in).

Anemone Particularly useful for brilliance of colour in spring. Plant in autumn 10 cm (4 in) apart and 5 cm (2 in) deep. For summer flowers delay planting until February. Good varieties of the single De Caen type include: 'Apennina' (sky blue), 'Hollandia' (large scarlet flowers), 'The Bride' (white). Probably most popular are the large-flowered semi-double St Brigid varieties such as 'Lord Lieutenant' (deep blue), 'The Admiral' (violet), 'The Governor' (scarlet). Heights 15–30 cm (6–12 in).

Chionodoxa (glory of the snow) One of the best early-flowering bulbs for March/April. Looks wonderful when naturalized in the lawn or as a carpet beneath deciduous shrubs and trees. Plant in clumps in autumn 5 cm (2 in) apart and 5 cm (2 in) deep. Most attractive is *C. luciliae*, sky blue with a large white centre. 'Alba' has large white flowers, 'Rosea' pure pink ones. The flowers are 2 cm (3/4 in) across on stems about 8 cm (3 in) high.

Colchicum (autumn crocus, meadow saffron or naked ladies) Flowers each autumn while leaves do not appear until late winter. Likes a deep soil and a sunny situation. Plant corms in August 7 cm (3 in) apart and 5 cm (2 in) deep. One of the best is *C. speciosum* 'Lilac Wonder', height of flowers 15 cm (6 in).

Eranthis (winter aconite) The very earliest flower of the year, arriving even before the snowdrops, with bright golden yellow flowers among

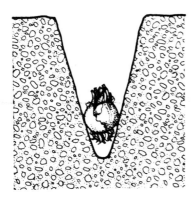

30 Bad planting
The deep, sloping sides will hinder drainage and encourage rot

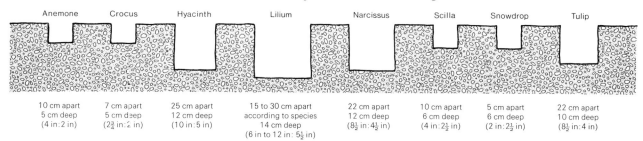

Anemone	Crocus	Hyacinth	Lilium	Narcissus	Scilla	Snowdrop	Tulip
10 cm apart	7 cm apart	25 cm apart	15 to 30 cm apart	22 cm apart	10 cm apart	5 cm apart	22 cm apart
5 cm deep	5 cm deep	12 cm deep	according to species	12 cm deep	6 cm deep	6 cm deep	10 cm deep
(4 in:2 in)	(2¾ in:2 in)	(10 in:5 in)	14 cm deep	(8½ in:4½ in)	(4 in:2½ in)	(2 in:2½ in)	(8½ in:4 in)
			(6 in to 12 in: 5½ in)				

31 Planting guide for bulbs

glossy bright green foliage. Does well on all types of soil and in all situations. Plant during August 5 cm (2 in) deep in groups of 8 to 10 and some 10 cm (4 in) apart. Height 15 cm (6 in).

Galanthus (snowdrop) Equally suitable for a sunny or shady place, will grow on all types of moisture-retentive soil. White flowers appear January/February. Plant 5 cm (2 in) apart and 6 cm (2½ in) deep. Height 7–25 cm (3–10 in).

Gladiolus Varieties which come into flower May/June are well worth growing as they give a brilliant splash of colour just as the last of the spring bulbs fade and continue until the summer bedding is planted out. Note that the larger-flowered gladioli flower late summer/early autumn. The early flowering kinds grow only 45–60 cm (18–24 in) high and corms are planted in autumn 10 cm (4 in) deep and 15 cm (6 in) apart. There are some splendid varieties such as 'Blushing Bride' (ivory white), 'Nymph' (white with a crimson fleck), 'Peach Blossom' (rosy pink), 'Spitfire' (scarlet) and 'Spring Glory' which is salmon pink with white blotches which in turn are surrounded with zones of crimson.

Leucojum (snowflake) At first sight looks rather like a giant snowdrop. The snow white flowers are green tipped, on stout stems 15 cm (6 in) high. *L. vernum* flowers February/March. Plant in autumn 8 cm (3 in) apart and 5 cm (2 in) deep.

Muscari (grape hyacinth) A beautiful little flower which will grow anywhere, even in shade. Looks best when planted in generous clumps and left undisturbed to multiply over the years. Flowers during April, height 15 cm (6 in). Plant in October 8 cm (3 in) apart and 10 cm (4 in) deep. Good varieties include *M. armeniacum* (bright blue fragrant flowers), *M. botryoides* (pale china blue), *M. botryoides* 'Album' (white), and *M. tubergenianum,* called 'Oxford and Cambridge' because the tops of its flowering spikes are clear blue while the lower regions are deep Oxford blue.

Scilla (squill) Very similar to *Chionodoxa*, and particularly valuable because its flowering period is February/March. Plant 10 cm (4 in) apart and 6 cm (2½ in) deep during early October. *S. bifolia* has deep blue flowers on stems 10 cm (4 in) high during February. *S. sibirica taurica* flowers February/March and has charming clear blue flowers.

A recommended selection of bulbs

HYACINTHS

	Height		Colour	Time of flowering	Bulb size	
	cm	in			cm	in
'Anne Marie'	15–22	6–9	light rose	March	17–18	7
'Carnegie'	15–22	6–9	pure white	April	17–18	7
'City of Haarlem'	15–22	6–9	primrose yellow	April	17–18	7
'Crown Princess Margaret'	15–22	6–9	soft pink	March/April	17–18	7
'Delft Blue'	15–22	6–9	porcelain blue	March	17–18	7
'Jan Bos'	15–22	6–9	carmine red	March	17–18	7
'Lady Derby'	15–22	6–9	salmon pink	March/April	17–18	7
'L'Innocence'	15–22	6–9	white	March	17–18	7
'Myosotis'	15–22	6–9	pale blue	March/April	17–18	7
'Ostara'	15–22	6–9	deep blue	March	17–18	7
'Pink Pearl'	15–22	6–9	rose pink	March	17–18	7
'Queen of the Pinks'	15–22	6–9	rose pink	April	17–18	7

The fragrance of hyacinths is exquisite and lasts several weeks. A truly outstanding display can be created in red, white and blue by using equal numbers of 'Delft Blue' and 'L'Innocence' and then planting in between each hyacinth *Tulipa praestans* 'Fusilier' which is orange red with some 3 to 5 flowers on a stem and grows some 20 cm (8 in) high.

TULIPS

	Height		Colour	Time of flowering	Bulb size	
	cm	in			cm	in
SINGLE EARLY TULIPS						
'Bellona'	40	16	golden yellow	mid-April	12	5
'Brilliant Star Maximus'	25	10	bright scarlet	early April	12	5
'General de Wet'	33	13	golden orange	early April	12	5
'Pink Beauty'	30	12	vivid pink	late April	12	5
'Van der Neer'	25	10	violet purple	mid-April	12	5
'Wintergold'	40	16	deep yellow	late April	12	5
DOUBLE EARLY TULIPS						
'Electra'	25	10	cherry red	mid-April	12	5
'Orange Nassau'	30	12	orange scarlet	mid-April	12	5
'Schoonoord'	30	12	pure white	mid-April	12	5
'Vuurbaak'	25	10	brilliant scarlet	late April	12	5
MENDEL TULIPS						
'Apricot Beauty,	40	16	rose salmon tinged apricot	late April	12	5
'Athleet'	45	18	pure white	late April	12	5
'John Gay'	35	14	warm orange red	late April	12	5
'Krelage's Triumph'	35	14	deep crimson red	late April	12	5
'Rijnsoever'	40	16	fine yellow	late April	12	5

A recommended selection of bulbs (contd)

	Height			Time of	Bulb size	
	cm	*in*	*Colour*	*flowering*	*cm*	*in*
TRIUMPH TULIPS						
'Alberio'	40	16	cherry red	early May	12	5
'Andes'	40	16	creamy white	early May	12	5
'Bingham'	45	18	golden yellow	early May	12	5
'Bruno Walter'	40	16	deep orange	early May	12	5
'Hibernia'	40	16	pure white	early May	12	5
'Lustige Witwe'	50	20	glowing deep red edged pure white	late April	12	5
'Paul Richter'	60	24	bright geranium red	early May	12	5
'Sulphur Glory'	55	22	creamy ivory	early May	12	5
DARWIN TULIPS						
'Clara Butt'	60	24	soft salmon pink	early May	12	5
'Cordell Hull'	60	24	bright red on a white ground	mid-May	12	5
'Duke of Wellington'	65	26	pure white	mid-May	12	5
'Mamasa'	52	21	bright yellow	early May	12	5
'Scarlet Sensation'	65	26	blood red	mid-May	12	5
DARWIN HYBRID TULIPS						
'Apeldoorn'	70	28	orange scarlet	early May	12	5
'Beauty of Apeldoorn'	70	28	golden yellow	early May	12	5
'Elizabeth Arden'	50	20	rose pink	mid-May	12	5
'Holland Glory'	65	26	bright scarlet	early May	12	5
'Oranje Sun'	40	16	pure orange	mid-May	12	5
'Striped Apeldoorn'	60	24	red striped yellow	early May	12	5
'Yellow Dover'	60	24	buttercup yellow	early May	12	5
COTTAGE TULIPS						
'Advance'	75	30	cherry red	early May	12	5
'Aster Nielsen'	65	26	sulphur yellow	mid-May	12	5
'G. W. Leak'	65	26	geranium red	mid-May	12	5
'Joan Cruickshank'	65	26	deep rose pink, lower half pure white	mid-May	12	5
'Mrs John T. Scheepers'	60	24	canary yellow	mid-May	12	5
'Princess Margaret Rose'	55	22	yellow flushed orange-red	late May	12	5
'Renown'	65	26	soft carmine red	mid-May	12	5
'White City'	70	28	pure white	mid-May	12	5
LILY FLOWERED TULIPS						
'Aladdin'	50	20	scarlet edged yellow	mid-May	12	5
'China Pink'	50	20	satin pink	early May	12	5
'Dyanito'	55	22	brilliant red	mid-May	12	5
'Golden Duchess'	58	23	deep yellow	mid-May	12	5
'Queen of Sheba'	60	24	glowing dark red edged orange	mid-May	12	5
'White Triumphator'	70	26	pure white	mid-May	12	5

A recommended selection of bulbs (contd)

	Height		Colour	Time of flowering	Bulb size	
	cm	*in*			*cm*	*in*
PARROT TULIPS						
'Black Parrot'	55	22	glossy purple black	mid-May	12	5
'Blue Parrot'	60	24	bluish purple	mid-May	12	5
'Doorman'	50	20	cherry red edged golden yellow	mid-May	12	5
'Fantasy'	55	22	salmon pink with emerald green markings	mid-May	12	5
'Orange Favourite'	55	22	orange with green marks	mid-May	12	5
'Texas Gold'	50	20	deep yellow edged red	mid-May	12	5
'White Parrot'	50	20	pure white	mid-May	12	5
BOTANICAL TULIPS						
Tulipa greigii 'Red Riding Hood'	20	8	bright scarlet	March	10–11	$4-4\frac{1}{4}$
Tulipa kaufmanniana 'Stresa'	25	10	Red, edged yellow	March	10–11	$4-4\frac{1}{4}$
Tulipa praestans 'Fusilier'	20	8	3 to 5 flowers per stem	April	10–11	$4-4\frac{1}{4}$

Herbaceous Borders

Your herbaceous border should be in a sunny position and away from overhanging trees, if at all possible. It should preferably be backed by a hedge or wall, to prevent strong winds breaking down the plants. Remember that hedge roots will extend anything up to a metre into the border area. When it comes to the question of soil, you have to make the best of what you have in the garden.

Preparing the ground

When preparing for a herbaceous border it is essential to cultivate the ground thoroughly two spits deep and incorporate plenty of bulky organic matter, for once the border is established it will be there for years. Make sure that all perennial weeds are cleared from the site at this stage, otherwise they will become a serious problem later. Use Dalapon to eradicate couch and other perennial grasses. Woody weeds can be controlled by ammonium sulphate (Amcide).

The actual planting season extends from October to March and it is advisable to start the ground works well in advance. If weeds have to be cleared first it will take time for the weed-killers to work. You should also allow time after cultivation for annual weeds to germinate and then, over several weeks, destroy them by hoeing. If you do this once or twice during the pre-planting period you will have a perfect border ready to receive the plants. Give a dusting of fish meal at the rate of 60 g per square metre (2 oz per square yard) and fork this into the surface prior to the planting season.

Planning your layout

Go around the plant nurseries during the summer and see for yourself what the various herbaceous perennials really look like. This will help you to plan pleasing associations of plants and it is the only way in which a beginner can clearly appreciate their size and form. In general the larger the border the larger the groups of plants should be. In a large border it is possible to plant in clumps of, say, 8 to 10 plants, but plant only 3 or 4 in a small one.

The space requirements of the plants within each clump will vary: the smallest will need perhaps no more than 23 cm (9 in) while the large ones at the back may well need upwards of 60 cm (2 ft) between them. Draw up a plan on paper, right at the very beginning, and work out exactly what is required. Do not plant in straight rows with the tallest at the back

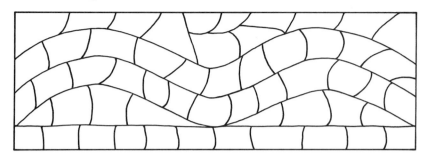

32 Transferring your plan for the border from paper to flower bed

Following your plan on paper, mark out the proposed planting scheme on the previously prepared ground with sand: avoid straight lines except with the small plants at the very front.

and the smallest at the front. It's far better to vary the layout a little by dividing the border into bays, with some of the taller growing varieties nearer the middle of the border and some of the smaller growing ones set in from the front between these promontories (see diagram 32).

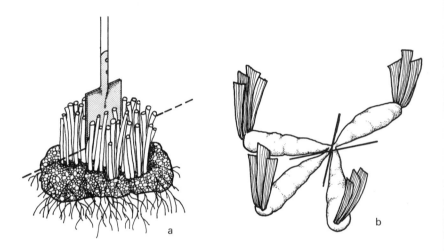

33 Splitting up established plants

a Using a spade to divide old clumps of fibrous plants is a quick and harmless method; the traditional way is to use a pair of garden forks
b A sharp knife should be used to divide iris rhizomes along the lines indicated

If you find it too costly to stock the whole border at once you could buy enough plants to complete only part of it and then in a couple of years stock up the remainder when it becomes necessary to split up the already established plants (see diagrams 33a and 33b). This splitting up will have to be undertaken anyway from time to time over the years, otherwise the established plants will simply grow into one another.

Planting

The best time to plant most herbaceous perennials is during October, but a few with fleshy roots and also delphiniums and pyrethrums are best planted in the spring (see diagram 34a). Those which you cannot plant at once should be kept damp until required. Make quite sure that fibrous rooted plants have their roots well spread out and that there is no

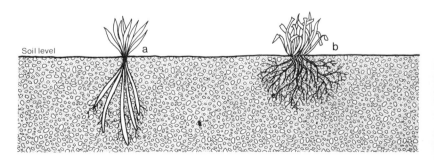

34 Planting methods

a Herbaceous plants with long fleshy roots should be planted at the appropriate depth with a spade
b Use a trowel to plant fibrous rooted plants; make sure that the roots are well spread out and the crowns barely 1 cm (about $\frac{1}{2}$ in) beneath the surface

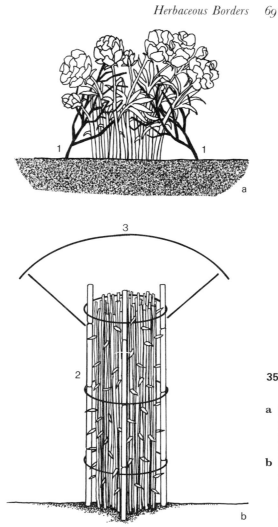

35 Unobtrusive support for herbaceous plants

a Short twiggy sticks (1) pressed into the ground provide the support needed by peonies; they will be hidden from view when the foliage develops

b Bamboo canes (2) placed in position when tall growing plants are still small should be a little shorter than the eventual height of the flowers (3) so as to be as inconspicuous as possible

cramping (see diagram 34b). On heavy soil it is a good idea to sprinkle a little coarse sand around the roots before drawing back the soil.

The plants should be so placed that their crowns are only a centimetre (half an inch) beneath the surface. Firm the soil back around them with your feet and then rake or point the surface with a garden fork to remove any foot marks.

After periods of severe frost check that none of the roots have been disturbed and if they have, firm them into position again.

Maintaining the herbaceous border

Each spring spread a mulch of peat, leaf mould or well rotted garden compost between the plants, for this keeps the roots cool and helps to preserve soil moisture and smother weeds. Use twiggy sticks to support bushy plants and stakes for the taller varieties (see diagrams 35a and 35b).

During the growing and flowering season remove dead flowers as required and shorten back early-flowering plants later in the season so that they do not spoil the appearance of the border. In the autumn first cut down all the dead remains of the plants to within 10 cm (4 in) of the ground and remove all the stakes. Then fork over the soil. Every third year lift and split up all the plants, discarding the older portions of the roots and replanting some of the new.

A selection of useful herbaceous perennials

Botanical name	Common name	Height cm	in	Time of flowering	Colours
Acanthus spinosus	bear's breeches	100	39	July–August	mauve
Achillea filipendulina 'Gold Plate'		150	60	June–August	bright yellow
A. millefolium 'Cerise Queen'	yarrow	70	28	June–August	deep red
Aconitum napellus 'Blue Sceptre'	monkshood	60	24	August–Sept	blue/white
Agapanthus campanulatus	African lily	60	24	July–Sept	powder blue
Anchusa azurea 'Morning Glory'		150	59	June–July	phenyl blue
A. azurea 'Loddon Royalist'		120	47	May–June	mid-blue
Anemone japonica 'Louise Uhink'	windflower	100	39	August–Oct	white
Anthemis sancti-johannis		75	30	July	bright orange
Aquilegia 'Crimson Star'	columbine	75	30	May–July	crimson and white
Aster amellus 'Sonia'	Michaelmas daisy	60	24	Sept	clear pink
A. novi-belgii 'Barton Royalist'		115	45	Sept–Oct	rose flushed red
A. novi-belgii 'Fellowship'		115	45	Sept–Oct	soft pink
A. novi-belgii 'Moderator'		120	47	Sept–Oct	deep violet purple
A. novi-belgii 'Orlando'		150	59	Sept–Oct	bright pink
A. novi-belgii 'Winston S. Churchill'		100	39	Sept–Oct	deep red
Astilbe 'Fanal'		60	24	June–August	dark crimson
A. 'Professor Van der Weilan'		100	39	June–August	white
A. 'Red Sentinel'		85	34	June–August	glowing red
Bergenia cordifolia		35	14	March–April	deep pink
Campanula glomerata	bellflower	45	18	June–July	purple
Chrysanthemum maximum 'Cobham Gold'	Shasta daisy	75	30	June–August	yellow
C. maximum 'Wirral Supreme'		90	36	June–August	white
Coreopsis grandiflora 'Mayfield Giant'		75	30	July–August	deep yellow
Delphinium (Belladonna Group)					
D. 'Blue Bees'		120	47	June–July	pale blue
D. 'Pink Sensation'		120	47	June–July	clear pink
D. 'Wendy'		120	47	June–July	gentian blue
D. (Elatum Group)					
D. 'Pacific Galahad'		150	59	June–July	pure white
D. 'Silver Moon'		150	59	June–July	silvery mauve
D. 'Wm. Richards'		150	59	June–July	electric blue
Dianthus (Border Carnations)	border carnation				
D. 'Cottage White'		45	18	June–July	white
D. 'Cottage Scarlet'		45	18	June–July	scarlet
D. 'Cottage Pride'		45	18	June–July	yellow marked crimson
Doronicum austriacum	leopard's bane	60	24	May	golden yellow
Echinacea purpurea 'The King'	purple cone flower	115	45	July–August	reddish purple
Echinops humilis 'Taplow Blue'	globe thistle	150	60	July–August	blue
Epimedium grandiflorum	barrenwort, bishop's hat	25	10	June	pale pink
Erigeron 'Charity'	fleabane	60	24	June–August	light pink
E. 'Dignity'		60	24	June–August	mauve-blue
E. 'Quakeress'		60	24	June–August	lavender blue
Geum 'Fire Opal'	avens	60	24	May–August	orange/flame
G. 'Lady Stratheden'		60	24	May–August	golden yellow
G. 'Mrs Bradshaw'		45	18	May–August	scarlet
Gypsophila 'Bristol Fairy'		120	47	July–Sept	white
G. 'Rosy Veil'		40	16	July–Sept	pale pink
Helenium 'Copper Spray'		60	24	July–Sept	orange gold
H. 'Moerheim Beauty'		110	43	July–Sept	rich crimson

A selection of useful herbaceous perennials (contd)

Botanical name	Common name	Height cm	in	Time of flowering	Colours
H. 'Riverton Gem'		150	59	July–Sept	red and gold
Helianthus decapitalus (multiflorus)					
'Loddon Gold'	sunflower	220	86	August–Oct	bright yellow
Heliopsis scabra 'Golden Plume'		120	47	July–Oct	golden yellow
Helleborus niger	Christmas rose	45	18	Dec–Feb	white
H. orientalis	Lenten rose	32	13	Nov–March	yellowy green
Heuchera 'Coral Cloud'	coral flower	45	18	June–Sept	coral red
H. 'Pearl Drops'		60	24	June–Sept	white
H. 'Red Spangles'		60	24	June–Sept	deep red
Hosta lancifolia albo-marginata	plantain lily	30	12	July–Sept	soft mauve
Incarvillea delavayi		30	12	June	rose red
Iris (Bearded)					
I. 'Blue Rhythm'		110	43	June	cornflower blue
I. 'Ethel Peckham'		95	38	May	clear red
I. 'Mattie Gates'		100	39	May	yellow and white
I. 'New Snow'		110	43	May	white
I. 'Radiant'		80	32	May	yellow and red
Kniphofia 'Bee's Lemon'	torch lily, red hot poker	115	45	July–Sept	chrome yellow
K. 'Fireflame'		100	39	July–Oct	orange scarlet
K. 'Maid of Orleans'		115	45	July–Sept	ivory white
K. 'Royal Standard'		100	39	July–Sept	yellow and scarlet
K. 'Sir C. K. Butler'		95	38	July–Sept	primrose yellow
Lobelia cardinalis 'Queen Victoria'		100	39	July–Sept	brilliant scarlet
Lupinus 'Billy Wright'	lupin	100	39	May–July	pink and white
L. 'Celandine'		100	39	May–July	clear yellow
L. 'Freedom'		100	39	May–July	lavender blue and white
L. 'Monkgate'		100	39	May–July	deep blue and white
Meconopsis bentonicifolia	Himalayan blue poppy	130	51	June	bright blue
Monarda 'Burgundy'	bergamot, horsemint	90	36	July–Sept	deep red
M. 'Melissa'		100	39	July–Sept	soft pink
Nepeta mussinii		30	12	May–Sept	lavender blue
Paeonia 'Queen Wilhelmina'	peony	75	30	June–July	vivid pink
P. 'Felix Crousse'		75	30	June–July	brilliant crimson
P. 'Marie Lemoine'		75	30	June–July	creamy white
Papaver orientale 'Lady Haig'	oriental poppy	90	36	June–July	warm scarlet
P. 'Storm Torch'		45	18	June–July	glowing red
Penstemon barbatus		75	30	July–August	coral red
Phlox paniculata 'Brigadier'		80	32	August–Sept	bright orange/red
P. 'Bright Eyes'		80	32	August–Sept	pink and cherry red
P. 'Eventide'		80	32	August–Sept	mauve
Polemonium coeruleum	Jacob's ladder, Greek valerian	60	24	July–August	bright blue
Polygonum amplexicaule	knotweed	80	32	August–Oct	rich crimson
Pyrethrum 'Brenda'		60	24	May–June	cherry pink
P. 'Evenglow'		60	24	May–June	reddish salmon
P. 'Scarlet Glow'		60	24	May–June	scarlet crimson
Rudbeckia 'Autumn Sun'	coneflower	190	75	August–Oct	yellow
R. 'Goldsturm'		60	24	July–Sept	orange yellow

A selection of useful herbaceous perennials (contd)

Botanical name	Common name	Height cm	in	Time of flowering	Colours
Salvia 'East Friesland'		40	16	June–July	violet blue
Scabiosa caucasica	scabious, pincushion				
S. 'Clive Greaves'		60	24	June–Oct	violet blue
S. 'Miss Willmot'		60	24	June–Oct	creamy white
Sedum spectabile 'Brilliant'		45	18	Sept–Oct	bright pink
S. 'Atropurpureum'		45	18	Sept–Oct	red
Solidago 'Goldenmosa'	goldenrod	75	30	August	yellow
S. 'Golden Wings'		180	71	Sept–Oct	yellow
S. 'Wendy'		45	18	August–Sept	yellow
Thalictrum aquilegifolium	meadow rue	90	36	May–June	pale purple
Tradescantia 'J. C. Weguelin'		60	24	June–July	azure blue
Trollius 'Earliest of All'	globe flower	40	16	May–June	yellow
T. 'Orange Princess'		40	16	May–June	bright orange
Verbascum 'C. L. Adams'	mullein	200	78	June–July	yellow
V. 'Cotswold Queen'		100	39	June–July	reddish brown
V. 'Gainsborough'		120	47	June–July	sulphur yellow
V. 'Pink Domino'		140	55	June–July	deep rose pink
Verbena bonariensis		130	51	June–July	lavender blue
Veronica incana	speedwell	30	12	June–August	dark blue
V. *teucrium* 'Royal Blue'		45	18	May–July	royal blue

You may decide to cover your garden with a hard surface for ease of maintenance (see pages 23–31). Crazy paving is always popular and has the additional charm of irregularity. The owner of this property has given life to his garden by means of large assorted tubs of bedding plants, shrubs, roses and climbers and an aviary which provides interest as well as colour.

Above: this sophisticated patio has the dual advantage of providing not only an area for growing plants, but, by virtue of the protection provided from the elements, an extension of the living area.

Right: no garden is too small to accommodate a pool of some sort. A correct balance between oxygenating plants and fish life should ensure the minimum of attention is required.

Window Boxes
and
Hanging Baskets

Window Boxes

Even a single window box can produce an amazing wealth of colour throughout the year. The flowers can be appreciated from both inside and outside the building, and they are easy to reach and care for.

Sash windows are best for window boxes since you have only to slide up the window to get at the box. Casement windows are a little more difficult because they open outwards, which means of course that nothing can be put on the sill in front of the section which opens. If one section is fixed, use a shorter box in the available space. If this is not feasible you can have wrought iron frameworks fixed to the wall beneath the window into which the boxes may be safely placed. Such an arrangement means that you can conveniently tend the plants, but of course they are less readily visible from indoors, as opening the window will damage the plants if they are tall enough to be seen. However, where the outward appearance of your home is your main consideration this would be of no great consequence.

To make or to buy?
All you need is a container some 20–25 cm (8–10 in) deep, 25 cm (10 in) wide and a convenient length to fit comfortably on your window sill. It will need to be secured by bolts into the wall, by hooks or by wire hoops. You can construct your own window boxes out of timber quite easily. Those made from oak or teak will last for many years, but the wood must be treated with a preservative. The most suitable kind is Cuprinol, for it is harmless to plant life. Creosote gives off fumes poisonous to plants.

Drill a number of drainage holes in the bottom of the box and screw wood blocks 3 cm ($1\frac{1}{4}$ in) square onto its base to lift it clear of the window sill. The box can then drain freely and air can circulate under it. This is important because the roots of plants require air as well as moisture to function properly (see diagram 36a).

Ready-made boxes come in various sizes and materials so with any luck you should be able to find one that will look right on your sill. Look

A good example of how paving can be broken up with ground cover plants and raised beds to achieve a varied and attractive appearance. The contrast between the colour and texture of the plant foliage is particularly effective.

36 Window boxes: points to check

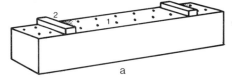

a 1 Make sure that there are plenty of
       drainage holes in the bottom
    2 Attach wood blocks to the base to lift
       it clear of the sill for free drainage

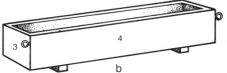

b 3 Provide means for securing window
       box into position safely and secure
       while still empty
    4 Apply a wood preservative such as
       Cuprinol—not creosote, which is
       harmful to plant life

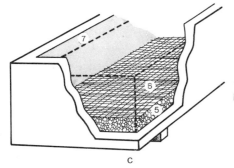

c 5 Put a drainage layer at the bottom
    6 Lay sacking over drainage layer
    7 Put in compost up to 3–4 cm
       ($1\frac{1}{4}$–$1\frac{5}{8}$ in) of the top; the space is
       essential to prevent any water that
       does not immediately soak in
       running off the surface

carefully at the box before you buy it. Has it got enough drainage holes?
If not, would it be difficult to make additional ones? Has it got 3 cm ($1\frac{1}{4}$in)
'legs' for drainage and air circulation? Finally, check the rigidity of the
box. If it bends when you press it, it is not going to keep its shape very
well when filled with any weight of compost.

Preparing the box

Secure the box into position while it is empty (see diagram 36b). Next, place
some broken crocks over the drainage holes. If you have no crocks you
can use washed shingle, which is easily obtainable from any builder at
little cost. This drainage layer should be 3–4 cm (about $1\frac{1}{2}$in) deep. On
top of it place a single thickness of sacking, which will prevent the
compost from being washed down into the shingle and blocking up its
drainage cavities. (See diagram 36c.)

Next add either John Innes Potting Compost or one of the soil-less
potting composts, lightly firmed and levelled to 3 cm ($1\frac{1}{4}$in) below the
top of the box. This space is essential, for if the compost was level with the
top of the box any water which did not soak in immediately would simply
run straight off the top and be lost to the plants.

Your window box round the year

Window boxes can usually produce two displays each year. They can be
colourful in spring with autumn-planted bulbs and again throughout the
summer when they are decked out with summer bedding plants.

However, if you are willing to go to the expense and the trouble, you
can use them simply as plant-pot containers and change the display more
frequently. In this case do not fill them with compost; place the potted
plants in the boxes and spread some sedge peat between them. This helps
to keep the roots cool in warm weather and also reduces evaporation.
When watering the plants give the peat a good soaking at the same time.

In the autumn short-stemmed chrysanthemums in an array of colours
can be put out in the boxes until they are destroyed by frost. They can
then be replaced by dwarf evergreen shrubs such as *Chamaecyparis*
(cypress) and its close relation *Cupressus*, or a winter-flowering heather
such as *Erica carnea*, which includes such beautiful varieties as 'King
George' with its carmine flowers, 'Ruby Glow' and 'Springwood White'.
The very delectable 'Vivellii' has the deepest red flowers of all and these
contrast impressively with its dark bronze winter foliage. Other possibilities are such evergreen shrubs as *Santolina* with its aromatic foliage,
Skimmia with its neat glossy leaves and bright red berries, and of course
Vinca (periwinkle).

The use of dwarf shrubs for winter display may at first seem very
extravagant, but these same pot plants can be used each winter, and
during the remainder of the year they can be sunk in the garden
complete with their pots or used on the patio, so they represent a very
worthwhile investment in the long term.

You can use pots of daffodils, hyacinths and tulips to replenish the
window boxes as soon as they begin to show colour, and augment these
with further pots of cinerarias, pansies, polyanthus and primroses.

Maintaining your window box

When growing plants directly in window boxes it is desirable to change
the compost once each year and at the same time renew the sacking over
the drainage layer. If left too long this will rot and thus become useless.

The compost can be made to serve a little longer by giving it a dressing of bone-meal but it is better to replace it with fresh material.

General maintenance consists of stirring the compost between the plants from time to time, to allow the free circulation of air and moisture around the roots of the plants and eradicate any weeds.

Water the boxes at 3 to 4 day intervals. In windy or sunny places they are likely to dry out more quickly.

Further plant food will be required after a time because the growing plants rapidly use up the nutrients in the existing compost, and some are also lost in the drainage water. To make good this loss it is advisable to supply a liquid feed once every 14 days during the summer, immediately after watering. Apply it in a weak solution only, otherwise excess foliage will be produced at the expense of flowers.

Remove dead flowers at frequent intervals to encourage continued flowering, and use short green split-canes to support the taller plants.

Planting recommendations

If you have the choice it is obviously an advantage to attach your boxes to the south side of your property where they will enjoy more sunshine, providing, of course, that no other higher property overshadows them. Usually however it is simply a question of choosing plants suitable for the aspect they are to occupy.

The following list of plants indicates the aspect to which each is best suited, while those plants which prefer shade are indicated by '(S)'.

Abutilon thompsonii South
Ageratum South and west
Albizzia All aspects (S)
Alyssum maritimum and *A. saxatile* (gold dust) All aspects except north
Antirrhinum (snapdragon) All aspects except north
Arabis caucasica All aspects except north
Asparagus sprengeri South, south east or south west
Aubrieta All aspects
Aucuba japonica (spotted laurel) Pot-grown, north, east and west (S)
Begonia (both tuberous rooted and fibrous rooted) All aspects except north (S)
Bellis perennis (common daisy) All aspects
Buxus sempervirens (common box) Pot-grown, all aspects (S)
Calceolaria South and west
Calendula (marigold) All aspects except north
Canna South and west
Celosia cristata (cockscomb) South and west
Cheiranthus (wallflower) All aspects except north
Chionodoxa (glory of the snow) All aspects
Chrysanthemum All aspects
Clarkia elegans All aspects except north
Convallaria majalis (lily of the valley) North and east (S)
Crocus All aspects
Dahlia All aspects except north
Dianthus (pinks and carnations) South and west
Fatsia japonica North east
Ferns North east and north west (S)
Fuchsia South west (S)
Geranium All aspects
Hedera helix (ivy) North east and north west
Hyacinthus All aspects
Impatiens (Busy Lizzie) All aspects (S)
Kochia South

Lavandula (lavender) South east and south west
Lobelia All aspects
Lysimachia nummularia (creeping jenny) All aspects except north (S)
Matthiola (stock) All aspects except north
Mesembryanthemum South west
Myosotis palustris (forget-me-not) All aspects (S)
Narcissus All aspects (S)
Nemesia South and west
Petunia South and west
Phlox drummondii South and west
Polyanthus All aspects (S)
Primula vulgaris (primrose) All aspects (S)
Salvia splendens South and west
Saxifraga umbrosa (London pride) All aspects
Sedum spectabile All aspects
Skimmia japonica (pot-grown) All aspects except north
Tagetes (marigold) All aspects
Tropaeolum majus and *minor* (nasturtium) All aspects
Tulipa All aspects
Verbena Hybrids, south
Zinnia South

Hanging Baskets

When properly planted up and cared for, hanging baskets give a great deal of pleasure all summer through. They often decorate front porches but are also used in conservatories, corridors and verandahs, where they can house more exotic plants than is possible in the open air. They are particularly useful for adorning otherwise drab walls in back yards, driveways, balconies, patios and roof gardens, and they do much to create an air of dignity and tranquillity. If the walls are dark coloured it is worth giving them a good coat of whitewash or pastel paint so that the baskets may be seen to better advantage.

Hanging baskets are available in galvanized wire, plastic-covered wire and toughened plastics. In general they measure 30–45 cm (12–14 in) across and are some 15–23 cm (6–9 in) deep. Suitable wall brackets are easily bought.

The larger the baskets the better they look when planted and the better they will accommodate a variety of plants. Avoid baskets which are less than 30 cm (12 in) across the top and less than 15 cm (6 in) deep because they hold too little compost to support the plants and enable them to grow satisfactorily.

Preparing the baskets
When filling the baskets support them on top of a bucket or suspended at a comfortable height. First they have to be lined to prevent the soil from being washed out and moss, obtainable from a good florist or nurseryman, is traditionally used for this purpose. Moisten it before putting it in and on top of it place a thin layer of turf, which helps to keep the moss moist and to retain the compost. Alternatively you can line the baskets with black plastic, and I strongly recommend this method, for plastic retains moisture more effectively and virtually eliminates the problem of drip. (See diagrams 37a and 37b.) Hanging baskets lose more water

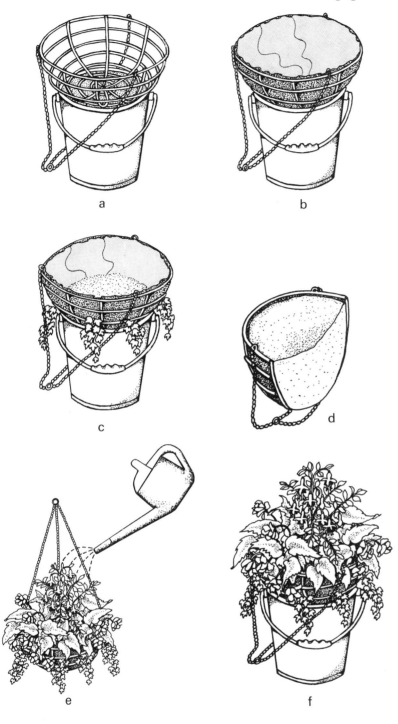

37 How to plant a hanging basket

The easiest way to brighten a drab courtyard or basement area.

a Stand the basket in a bucket
b Line the basket with black plastic, then trim round the top with a pair of scissors
c Insert plants through the sides of the basket while in the process of filling it with compost—use the blade of a knife to make small holes in the plastic
d A half-section of the basket, showing a $3–4\,\mathrm{cm}$ ($1\tfrac{1}{2}$–$1\tfrac{5}{8}$ in) depression in the compost after it has been filled, to prevent overflow when watering
e Remember to feed the basket with liquid fertilizer every 14 days
f The completed basket ready for hanging

through evaporation than either window boxes or tubs, and plastic-lined baskets, while still calling for a fair amount of attention, are far less exacting than those lined with moss.

Use either John Innes Compost No 2 or one of the soil-less composts such as J. Arthur Bowers' or Levington. Make certain you ask for potting compost, because other composts are sold for different purposes.

Insert the plants in the baskets before they are full of compost and firm the roots in well with your hands as the work proceeds. With moss-lined baskets it is customary to plant some of the smaller trailing plants not only around the rim but also in through the sides of the basket. You just poke a hole with your fingers and slot the roots of the plant through as the filling progresses. Plastic-lined baskets can be treated in exactly the same manner but you have to cut a hole in the plastic with a knife, taking care not to make it larger than necessary. (See diagram 37c.)

The finished surface of the basket should be nudging the top of the rim all the way round, but in the middle the compost should be 3–4 cm ($1\frac{1}{2}$ in) lower (see diagram 37d). This hollow holds the water each time that watering takes place, preventing an immediate overflow.

To keep the plants bearing flowers throughout the summer you must supplement the compost by adding liquid fertilizer every 14 days, and it is good practice to remove all dead or dying flowers at the same time (see diagram 37e).

Suitable plants for hanging baskets
For hanging in the open, baskets are planted up (see diagram 37f) during May and early June, according to the district. They should be hung outside only when all fear of frost has passed. Suitable plants include *Alyssum*, *Begonia* (both fibrous and tuberous varieties), *Calceolaria*, *Centaurea*, *Coleus* (very useful for its foliage), *Fuchsia* (particularly the pendulous varieties) and *Heliotropium*. *Impatiens* (Busy Lizzie) in mixed colours makes a truly outstanding display all on its own the whole summer through, in sun or shade. Other suitable plants include *Lobelia* (particularly the cascading varieties), both the upright and creeping varieties of *Pelargonium* (incorrectly called geranium), *Petunia*, *Phlox* (particularly the dwarf bedding varieties), *Salvia*, *Tradescantia*, *Tropaeolum* (nasturtium) and the dwarf trailing varieties of *Verbena*.

If the baskets are to be hung in a greenhouse, verandah or other sheltered place the planting potentialities are increased still further. Such plants as *Begonia haageana*, *Columnea banksii*, *Plectranthus oertendahlii* and many more can be used. One basket could accommodate *Columnea gloriosa* 'Purpurea', which is covered with orange-red flowers in the late spring, and another could hold *Hoya bella*, a slender drooping evergreen which bears masses of waxy clusters of small white flowers with either a red or purple centre. Early forced bulbs are useful during the winter and in the late autumn you could display the ten-week *Chrysanthemum*.

Although hanging baskets are chiefly used during the summer there is no reason why you should not use them the whole year through, for in the autumn they can be planted up with spring flowering bulbs together with some hardy perennials which will provide a focus of attraction during the winter. The small-leaved ivy *Hedera helix* 'Hibernica' and *Vinca minor* (lesser periwinkle) are a couple of very accommodating perennials for winter decoration, since neither is affected by lack of sunshine.

When replanting the baskets, empty them out and introduce fresh compost. Bulbs such as crocus, grape hyacinth, tulip, etc, are planted as the compost is put in, with their tips pointing out through the sides and top of the basket.

If you are planting daffodils choose the short-stemmed and miniature kinds, so that they will be able to withstand the wind. If you want tulips choose the short-stemmed Botanical Tulips for these flower much earlier than others and over an extended period. Furthermore they will flower year after year as long as you plant them out in the garden until the following autumn, when they may be dug up once more for replanting.

Roses for the Town Garden

The rose grows happily in all parts of the country and upon a wide range of soils. It is ideally suited to towns as it is not easily injured by atmospheric pollution.

Where and when to plant roses

Contrary to general belief roses do not prefer heavy clay soil. A medium to heavy loam is much more to their liking, but both heavy and light types are satisfactory if they are of a reasonable depth. They should be given a generous dressing of manure or well rotted garden compost and then be thoroughly cultivated. The roses are likely to remain in the soil for many years, so it is important to give them the best start possible. Roses do best in an open position, but this is not always easy to find in our smaller town gardens. However, there should be no problem as long as you do not plant them under trees in constant shade.

The planting season is from November to March whenever the weather is favourable. It is a mistake to disturb snow and ice simply to get the roses into the ground, for any frosted soil which is buried will prevent the soil warming up in spring and retard the root action. The ideal planting time is immediately after leaf fall. Make sure that your plants arrive at the right time by placing an order with a reputable rose grower not later than June.

How to plant roses

If the roses are to have a bed to themselves rake down the soil to produce a suitable crumb structure and then mark out each row with a garden line. The planting distances of bush roses will depend on the vigour of the individual plants, but with most kinds a distance of 50 cm (20 in) will do just fine, while the more vigorous ones will need about 75 cm (30 in) in both directions. Your aim is to plant them so that their foliage shades their roots.

Diagrams 38a–e illustrate how to handle the bushes on arrival. If any plants are damaged prune them back with secateurs. Dig a hole large enough to accommodate the roots without cramping, and ensure that the union between the root stock and budding point is just above ground level. Hold the rose upright in the hole and gradually work the soil down between the roots with a spade, shaking the bush lightly. Firm it into position with your foot. Once all the roses are planted dress the soil with bone meal at the rate of 60 g per square metre (2 oz per square yard) and rake it into the surface.

38 Planting a rose bush

a Unpack the rose on arrival
b Soak it in water before planting out if it
   has had to be stored in a frost-free place
c Prune any damaged roots
d As the soil is replaced in the hole, shake
   the bush lightly to work the soil down
   between the roots
e Check that the soil level is correct—the
   union between the rootstock and
   budding point should be just above
   ground level; then firm the soil with the
   feet

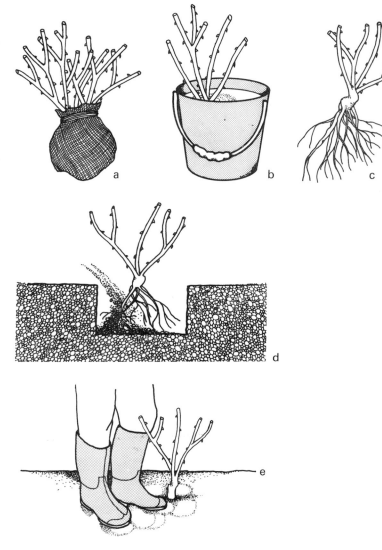

If the rose bushes arrive when the weather is unsuitable simply loosen
the packing so that air can reach the roots, and keep them in a cool, frost-
free place until conditions improve. They can be kept for many weeks if
necessary, but you must soak the roots in water for 24 hours before
planting them out.

Frost and gales are liable to loosen the roots of newly planted roses, so
check from time to time and firm any which need attention, otherwise
the stems will chafe and the damage could result in their ultimate death.
Water too may gather in the holes caused by wind rock and can be a
further cause of mortalities.

Daffodils may be under-planted in rose beds and will provide a useful
early display during March and April. A carpet of *Campanula isophylla*
(bellflower) will produce masses of steel blue flowers over many months,
and its low foliage effectively prevents the growth of weeds. The cool
shady environment provided by the roses is entirely to its liking.

Pruning

Do not begin to prune established rose bushes before the beginning of
March, and leave newly planted ones until they begin to show some signs

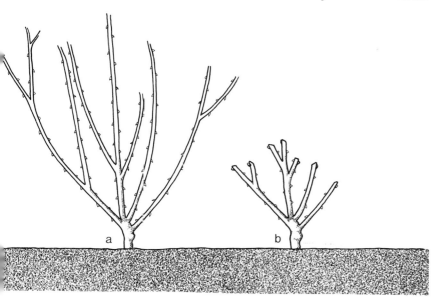

39 Pruning a vigorous hybrid tea rose

a, b Before and after pruning. This is a
modified form of 'long' pruning
which can be used on vigorous
hybrid tea roses to encourage them to
make taller bushes. It is more suited
to plants in borders rather than beds

of life during April. All dead and diseased wood should be removed and
the remainder pruned back to an outward-facing bud some 3 to 5 buds
from the base of the bush (see diagrams 39a and 39b). This will form an
open-centred bush with free circulation of air. Make the cut just above
each bud, leaving no snags of wood (see diagrams 40a–c).

Newly planted roses need pruning back hard to 3 buds the first year
and weak-growing established roses should receive the same treatment,
for this is the only way to encourage vigorous growth. Prune standard
roses in the same way as bush roses. To prune floribunda roses see
diagrams 41a and 41b.

Newly planted rambling roses should be severely pruned during
March and April. Choose three of the strongest shoots and cut them back
to approximately 45 cm (18 in) while reducing the remainder to a couple
of buds from the base. During the first season of growth new shoots are
produced from the base. Retain the best of these in the autumn and
prune the rest hard back to the base.

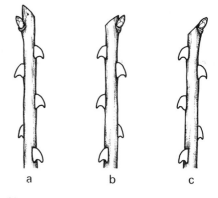

40 Examples of good and bad pruning

a Bad—the cut has been made too high
above the bud; the section will die back
to the bud and any infection which
may gain entry may kill the branch or
even the whole bush

b Good; the cut is correctly made

c Bad—the cut has been made too close
to the bud which will cause this bud to
die, affecting the branch as well back to
the next bud underneath

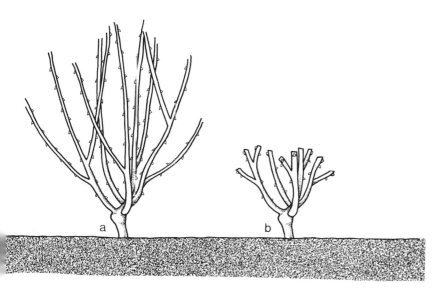

41 Pruning floribunda roses

a, b Before and after pruning

42 Pruning established rambler roses

a The season's growth before pruning
b The ties cut and the new and old
    growth sprawling on the ground
c Cutting away the old growths at the
    base and retaining the best of the new
d New growths secured to stake

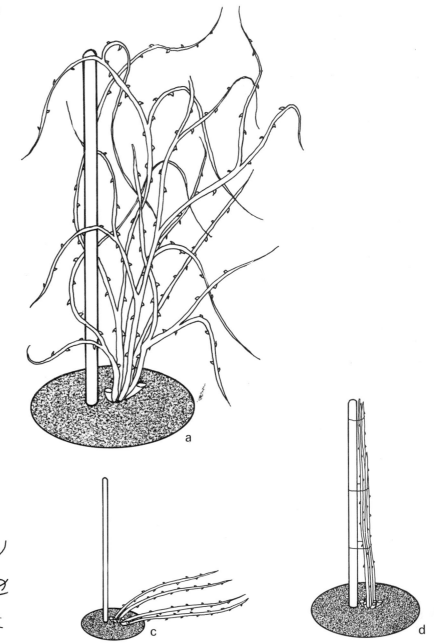

Established rambler roses are autumn pruned each year immediately after they have finished flowering (see diagram 42a). Cut all the ties and let the rambler sprawl out over the ground (see diagram 42b). If sufficient new shoots have been produced select the best 5 or 6 for tying to the support again and then prune back to ground level all the old wood together with any unwanted new growth (see diagram 42c). There is usually some soft sappy growth and this should never be retained. New shoots which are to be tied in should be about 180 cm (71 in) long and consist of ripened wood. If they have soft shoots at the tips prune them back a little to remove these, then secure the plants to their supports once again (see diagram 42d). If little new growth has been produced then retain the best of the current season's flowering wood, pruning out all the remains of the flowering trusses.

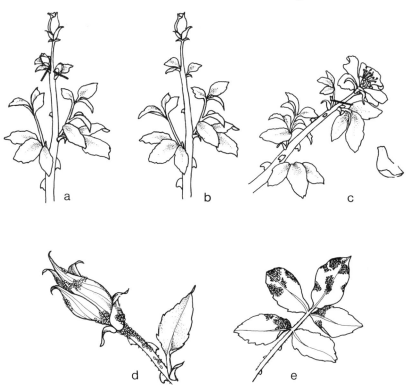

43 Maintaining established rose beds

a Disbudding: a hybrid tea rose which would benefit from disbudding

b The two side buds have been removed and the remaining bud will produce a larger and better flower

c Deadheading: dead blooms should be removed, cutting right back to a leaf joint with another bud, as it is from this that the next bloom or truss will be produced

d Pest and disease control: aphids and other sap-sucking insects are a serious problem; treat with Malathion or with a systemic insecticide such as Demeton-S-methyl to control them

e The characteristic features of Black Spot, a serious fungus disease; use Captan and Maneb to control

Climbing roses do not grow so vigorously as ramblers. They are planted to cover walls or fences, and until they have done so no pruning is called for. Even then simply remove the occasional unwanted growth and dead or diseased wood.

Maintaining established rose beds

Both new and established roses benefit from a mulching with rotted manure or grass cuttings every spring, immediately after pruning. Fork the soil over, then apply the mulch to the surface about 4 cm ($1\frac{1}{2}$ in) thick, taking care to prevent it coming into direct contact with the base of the roses. In the autumn apply bone-meal at the rate of 60 g per square metre (2 oz per square yard) and then work the remains of the mulch into the top 6–8 cm ($2\frac{1}{2}$–3 in) of soil.

In the spring you can improve the size of hybrid tea rose blooms by disbudding them (see diagrams 43a and 43b).

Summer work consists of controlling weeds, removing suckers, removing blooms as they fade (see diagram 43c), top-dressing with dried blood and keeping a sharp lookout for mildew. Benomyl is a very effective method of controlling mildew and should be applied at the first signs of attack. Black spot is controlled by Captan, and rose aphids by Malathion. (See diagrams 43d and 43e.)

Roses for town gardens

Do not simply choose rose trees from a glossy catalogue; visit one or more rose nurseries and see them growing for yourself. The following selection consists of varieties which have stood the test of time and can be relied on to give a good display each summer.

A selection of roses

Name of rose	Height cm	in	Colour and scent
HYBRID TEA ROSES			
REDS			
Crimson Glory	90	36	Bright velvety crimson and of considerable fragrance
Josephine Bruce	75	30	Rich blood red with velvety dark shadows
Uncle Walter	60	24	Scarlet shading crimson
Wendy Cussons	90	36	Rosy red with a pale pink reverse; scented
PINKS			
Princess Margaret	75	30	Glowing pink
Silver Lining	75	30	Silver pink and very fragrant
The Doctor	75	30	Rich pink with strong fragrance
LAVENDERS			
Blue Moon	80	32	Clear lavender with considerable fragrance
Sterling Silver	60	24	Silver lavender with a fair fragrance
YELLOWS			
Buccaneer	100–120	39–47	Buttercup yellow; moderate scent
Grandpa Dickson	90	36	Lemon yellow
Peace	150	59	Yellow edged delicate pink
Spek's Yellow	90	36	Rich yellow with a slight scent
BICOLORS			
Harry Wheatcroft	90	36	Orange striped and splashed yellow
Piccadilly	75	30	Red and yellow
Rose Gaujard	90	36	Deep pink/red with silvery pink reverse
Tzigane	60	24	Bright scarlet with chrome yellow reverse; moderate fragrance
WHITES			
Message	60	25	White with greenish shading at the base; moderate scent
Virgo	75	30	Pure white
FLORIBUNDA (HYBRID POLYANTHA) ROSES			
REDS			
City of Belfast	60	24	Orange scarlet
Evelyn Fison	75	30	Bright scarlet
Frensham	90	36	Deep crimson
PINKS			
City of Leeds	120	47	Salmon pink; slight scent
Dainty Maid	75	30	Carmine and pink
Queen Elizabeth	150	59	Clear pink with Hybrid Tea-like blooms
YELLOWS			
Allgold	60	24	Deep yellow
Arthur Bell	90	36	Bright yellow; moderate fragrance
Golden Treasure	80	32	Golden yellow; fragrant
Yellow Queen Elizabeth	120	47	Pale yellow

Name of rose	Height cm	in	Colour and scent

Floribunda (hybrid polyantha) roses *(contd)*

MULTICOLOUR

Circus	90	36	Colour constantly changing from yellow to pink and finally salmon/orange
Masquerade	90	36	Yellow, pink and deep red

WHITES

Iceberg	120	47	Snow white
Yvonne Rabier	120	47	White; moderate fragrance

CLIMBING ROSES

REDS

Ena Harkness	—	Crimson, scarlet; fragrant
Etoile de Holland	—	Dark red; considerable fragrance

PINKS

Shot Silk	—	Bright pink; moderate fragrance

ORANGES

Mrs Sam McGredy	—	Deep salmon orange flushed red; fragrant
Super Star	—	Light vermillion; fragrant

YELLOWS

Gloire de Dijon	—	Rosy buff; fragrant
Spek's Yellow	—	Bright yellow; slight scent

WHITES

City of York	—	Creamy white; fragrant

RAMBLING ROSES

MIXED COLOURS

Albertine	—	Copper orange fading salmon pink; fragrant
American Pillar	—	Red with a white eye
Crimson Shower	—	Brilliant crimson
Emily Gray	—	Golden yellow
New Dawn	—	Shell pink
Paul's Scarlet Climber	—	Bright scarlet

A Private Place: Hedges and Screens

Hedges shelter your garden and give you more privacy. They provide a good backcloth for the bright colours of other plants, and can be arranged as screens to block out less pleasant features inside and outside your garden: the compost heap, ugly buildings, and so on.

Hedges are much cheaper than walls or fences, and cost very little to maintain. They are better for your garden, too, because they create much less wind turbulence. However, walls and fences are quickly erected while hedges must slowly grow to the right size. Some plants grow much more rapidly than others; even so you must realize that what will ultimately prove to be your ideal hedge will call for some patience on your part. Make sure that the plants you choose are well furnished to ground level with branches; avoid leggy plants with bare lower stems. The shape in which you trim a formal hedge may affect the growth of the hedging plants used (see diagrams 44a–c).

In addition to straightforward hedges, some climbers will also make useful screens if you provide them with trellis-work or some other similar support. You might consider *Clematis*, *Lonicera* (honeysuckle), *Polygonum* (knotweed), *Wistaria*, and climbing or rambling roses.

Preparing your site

Before planting hedges dig the ground two spits deep and incorporate a good dressing of manure, garden compost, well rotted grass cuttings, leaf mould, etc (see diagram 45a). Remember your hedge will be there for many years and these preparations are essential to the proper establishment and active growth of the plants. If the site is low lying and badly

44 Formal hedges

a, b These are nicely shaped plants and a good, well-furnished hedge will result

c A poor shape; the lower part of such a hedge would lose its leaves and become bare due to lack of light

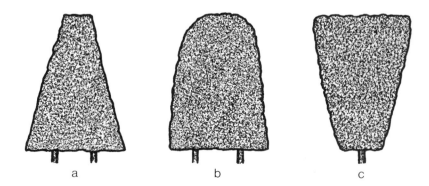

a   b   c

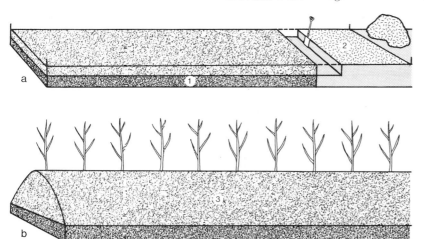

45 Preparing the site
a 1 Dig the ground two spits deep
  2 Incorporate manure or compost
b 3 If the ground is badly drained, make
    a bank of earth in which to plant

drained, either provide drainage or throw up a bank of earth and plant on top of it (see diagram 45b). These preparations should be completed well in advance of planting so that the soil has time to settle down again.

Planting hedges

Deciduous hedging plants are best planted in the autumn immediately after leaf fall. They can of course be planted throughout the winter, especially during February and March, provided that the soil is neither too wet nor frosty. However, over the years I have found that with autumn planting the roots have time to establish themselves long before bud movement begins, and fewer losses result.

Evergreens need even more care. They give off moisture from their leaves the whole year round, and this water must be replaced continuously if they are to survive. You can plant evergreens in September but the best time is April or early May, when the air is moist and the soil is warming up a little. To improve your chances you can spray the leaves, immediately after planting, with a solution such as S-600 which will greatly reduce the loss of moisture. Showery weather is a great aid to establishment but if the weather is dry you can help by spraying the leaves with water each morning as well as watering the soil if necessary.

Thrust your hand down beneath the surface of the soil to discover whether it is drying out. Soil can be very deceiving; it can be very dry on top and yet be quite moist beneath the surface. Any watering of evergreens should be done thoroughly, for just damping the surface simply encourages the production of surface roots which in continued dry weather soon shrivel and die. On the other hand over-watering will cause the soil to become waterlogged and cold, inhibiting the growth of the roots or even killing them.

46 Planting a hedge
a An example of good planting; the plants in this double row are positioned so that those in the second row alternate with those in the first row
b Reminders:
  1 Look for the earth stain on the stem of each hedging plant and replace it at the correct depth
  2 Tread the ground firm round base of each plant as planting progresses
  3 Rake the soil to remove footmarks on completion

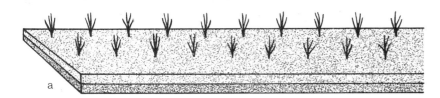

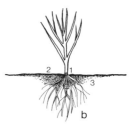

The planting procedure for hedges is outlined in diagrams 46a and 46b. See to it that you dig holes of sufficient size to accommodate the existing root balls comfortably; the distance apart depends on the size of the plants and how quickly you want them to become established. Take care that each plant is at the same depth as it was before transplanting. Damaged roots will rot; cut them back with a sharp knife, and new roots will be thrown out to replace them. Firm the soil around the roots so that the shrub is firmly anchored and the soil is of the same degree of compaction as that in the root ball itself. Moisture will then permeate the root ball readily and not simply drain away, which is one of the most common causes of shrubs failing. A top-dressing of peat or grass mowings, applied after a thorough watering, will help to keep the soil moist and discourage weeds.

Recommended plants for hedges and screens

DECIDUOUS

Acer campestre (field maple) Grows very freely almost everywhere; is widely used for hedges. Young foliage is maroon in spring, yellow in autumn. Plant 50 cm (20 in) apart and trim during winter. Height 2–3 m (6–10 ft). As a tree this plant forms a round head and grows to about 7 m (23 ft).

Artemisia abrotanum (southernwood, lad's love) A small erect aromatic shrub with feathery grey-green foliage. Makes a low informal hedge up to 1 m (3 ft 3 in) when allowed to grow freely. Plant 38–45 cm (15–18 in) apart. Clipping, if any, best done in spring before new growth commences.

Berberis (barberry) *B. thunbergii* is very useful for formal hedges. It responds well to clipping, but takes a little time to get established. Adorned with light yellow flowers in spring and bright red berries in autumn, when the leaves also turn brilliant red and scarlet. Plant at intervals of 60 cm (2 ft). Grows to 1.3 m (4 ft 3 in). Trim once annually to make a compact, impenetrable, spiny barrier. *B. wilsonae* forms a dense mound of spiny stems with soft, almost evergreen, foliage which turns red and orange in autumn with clusters of orange red berries. In spring it has deep golden flowers. Grows to 1 m (3 ft 3 in) and if unrestricted spreads about 1.5 m (4–5 ft). *B. vulgaris* is better in exposed positions and makes a fine informal screen up to 2.5 m (8 ft). It is covered with yellow flowers in May/June and in autumn produces clusters of translucent red berries with red and orange foliage.

Fagus sylvatica (common beech) Has long been popular for hedging. Its brown leaves persist through the winter providing it is not clipped later than August. Plant 45–60 cm (18–24 in) apart. Succeeds in most soils except heavy clays and can be grown to make quite tall shelter hedges.

Fuchsia magellanica 'Riccartonii' Makes a delightful informal hedge in milder coastal districts and even when cut down to the ground by frost soon grows up once more, making strong annual growth in any well drained soil. Plant 30 cm (12 in) apart. Produces scarlet and purple flowers from June to late September.

Potentilla fruticosa (shrubby cinquefoil) Some varieties are ideal for formal hedges, growing quite happily in any soil in a sunny situation. When once established no attention is necessary, and they flower continuously from May to September. Height about 1.5 m (4–5 ft). Plant about 45 cm (18 in) apart. Recommended: 'Farrer's White', 'Golden Drop', 'Sunset' (orange).

Rosa Floribunda roses are useful for informal hedges, especially 'City of Leeds', 'Frensham', 'Masquerade' and 'Queen Elizabeth'.

EVERGREEN

Berberis (barberry) Many evergreen varieties make excellent hedges, and all are spiny. Plant 45 cm (18 in) apart. *B. darwinii* is very attractive, with bright orange flowers in April/May and small holly leaves. *B. gagnepainii* makes a neat and quite impenetrable hedge. Yellow flowers, narrow crinkled leaves. Clipping is optional and best done immediately flowering ceases.

Buxus (box) Easily grown on all types of soil and equally at home in sun or shade 'Handsworthensis' is the most popular variety. Plant 30–38 cm (12–15 in) apart. Clip in spring and again in August.

Cotoneaster simonsii A semi-evergreen which will grow in any situation and on a wide range of soils. Plant 30–38 cm (12–15 in) apart. Bears bright red berries from autumn well into winter. Responds well to clipping.

Cupressocyparis leylandii (Leyland cypress) Has grey-green foliage, is fast growing and extremely hardy. Plant 45–60 cm (18–24 in) apart. Unequalled for tall hedges, especially in coastal districts, for it is tolerant of poor soils, exposed situations and salt-laden air. Responds well to clipping.

Hebe For mild and coastal districts there are several species very suitable for low hedges. No special soil preference but as long as it is well drained it will survive where many other shrubs fail. *H. salicifolia* has bright green foliage and drooping spikes of white or lilac flowers from June to August and withstands most winters. Plant 60 cm (2 ft) apart.

Ilex aquifolium (common holly) Beautiful throughout the year; makes a good barrier against intruders. Very hardy and grows on a wide range of soils. Plant 60 cm (24 in) apart. Clip in a somewhat pyramidal shape to encourage leaves right down to the base.

Pyracantha crenulata (firethorn) Hardy, vigorous and thorny, particularly suitable for a boundary hedge. Plant 50 cm (20 in) apart. Covered in little white flowers in spring and in the autumn with bright red berries which last well into February.

Climbers to Clothe the Walls

Towns and cities contain an amazing amount of unrelieved brick and stone which can be downright depressing to look at. Yet with a few climbing plants you can transform the walls in your garden, or at the front of your house, softening the harshness and adding an air of sophistication to the most unpromising property.

If you have enough space for a trench you can grow climbers quite successfully. Where there is a path against the wall you can clear a space by chopping through it and through the hardcore beneath. If the property is not your own, however, it is best to use tubs and leave the hard surface undisturbed. First position the tubs and then fill them with topsoil and fertilizer. Remember that any repairs to your walls must be completed before planting.

Preparing your site

Dig out a trench 30 cm (12 in) wide and about 60 cm (24 in) deep, adding some decent topsoil if none is already there. If available incorporate some well rotted farmyard manure or equally rotted lawn mowings, but bury it well below the surface so that the roots do not come directly into contact with it at planting time (see diagram 47). A good root run is essential, so if possible dig the soil over 2 spits deep. When returning the top spit break it up to give a fine crumb structure and then spread some fine sedge peat 2.5 cm (1 in) thick over the surface. Work it into the top 15 cm (6 in) of soil with a garden fork.

Finally dust over the surface 30 g (1 oz) of coarse bone meal for each plant and fork this into the top few centimetres of soil to stimulate the growth of the roots. During the first year or two the young climbers are most susceptible to drought and it is very important to encourage them to develop roots rapidly.

Water the ground thoroughly several days before planting and again immediately after planting is completed. Put down a mulch of peat after watering to help keep the roots cool and prevent evaporation.

Some climbers need the support of wall nails and wire or trellis (see diagrams 48 and 49), while others are self clinging (e.g. virginia creeper, see diagram 50). They are all sold with supporting canes and these must be left with them when planted. With twining climbers the cane should be close to the supports already on the wall so that the plant has no difficulty in gaining a firm hold.

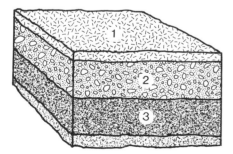

47 Cross-section of planting trench

1 Peat mulch on the surface to conserve moisture
2 Double-dug soil, with manure or compost incorporated into lower spit
3 Subsoil loosened with garden fork for good root run

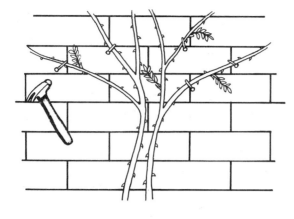

48 Wall nails securing a climbing rose

Recommended climbers

None of the plants listed below will cause any damage; they will in fact help protect the walls from weathering. All need some support (see preparation above) unless otherwise indicated.

Actinidia A hardy climber, rather unusual in appearance. *A. chinensis* (Chinese gooseberry) bears gooseberry-shaped fruits up to 5 cm (2 in) long. The fragrant flowers are cup shaped and cream coloured. *A. kolomikta* is more slender with leaves which are first green, then streaked with white, finally partly pink.

Chaenomeles (flowering quince) Thrives on north or east facing walls. When planted facing south will very often flower in a mild winter. Choose 'Knap Hill Scarlet' or 'Rowallane Seedling'.

49 Wall supports
a Trellis support correctly mounted:
   1 Trellis
   2 Climbing plant
   3 Cane
b Sideview of trellis
   4 Wall
   5 Wooden blocks keeping trellis clear of the wall's surface
c Plastic climbing support, wooden laths serving the same purpose

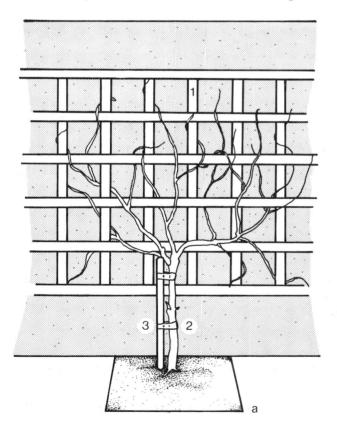

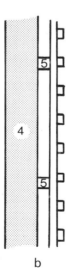

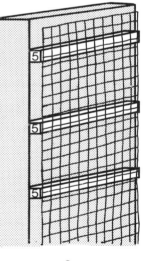

50 Water conservation

A self-clinging climber, such as Virginia creeper, benefits from pieces of paving stone being placed on the soil to help conserve moisture around the roots

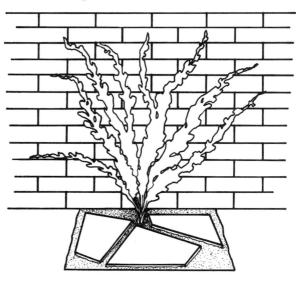

Chimonanthus (winter sweet) Likes well drained soil and a south facing wall. Grow it near a window for in summer it is clothed with long green scented leaves and in winter with equally fragrant flowers.

Clematis Colours range from white to almost red with some wonderful shades of blue and purple. It will even climb over shrubs, producing a most attractive result. Grow on a north or west facing wall, preferably in a light peaty soil. By choosing your varieties carefully you can have blossom from April to late September. My favourites are 'Nellie Moser' (striped mauvish pink; flowers May/June and again in September) and 'Ville de Lyon' (bright carmine; flowers from July to October).

Cotoneaster A very hardy shrub which flourishes in cold sunless situations and in nearly any soil providing drainage is satisfactory. Varieties range from evergreen to deciduous, with white or pink flowers in spring and yellow, orange or red berries in autumn. I recommend *C. lacteus*, the only full evergreen, with deep-green oval leaves which show up the white flowers during June and bunches of orange-red fruits which colour late and normally persist throughout the winter.

Forsythia suspensa Long pendulous shoots covered in spring with bright yellow flowers.

Hedera (ivy) Varieties are not all equally vigorous so be careful about your choice. The following hardy evergreens are of relatively rapid growth, respond well to clipping and thrive in almost any soil or situation: *H. canariensis* 'Variegata' (deep green leaves edged in silver and white). A hardier variety is *H. colchica dentata* 'Aurea' (large elongated leaves, bright green shading to grey with creamy yellow or white pronounced variegations).

H. helix 'Caenwoodiana' (small 3-lobed dark green leaves; grows quite happily where little else will succeed). *H. helix poetica* (Italian ivy) has beautiful bright green shallow-lobed leaves which in winter often turn bright copper.

Hydrangea petiolaris Suitable for any aspect. Self clinging; carries flat heads of white flowers as big as saucers which completely cover it during June/July.

Jasminum nudiflorum (winter jasmine) Thrives anywhere, though better to avoid an eastern aspect for the flowers are more likely to suffer if first frosted and then exposed to direct sun. Covered with bright yellow flowers from late autumn to March/April.

Lonicera (honeysuckle) Not at its best on a wall; prefers old trees, rustic poles, pergolas, fences. Most spectacular is *L. americana* with most beautiful sprays about 30 cm (12 in) long crowded with fragrant flowers, first white, then yellow, finally flushed rose. Flowers from June to September and is a vigorous grower.

Magnolia grandiflora 'Exmouth' A perfectly hardy evergreen with polished leaves 30–35 cm (12–14 in) long which completely cover any wall. Bears large richly scented flowers of a creamy white between July and September. Best planting time is spring because it is subject to root damage and decay if moved when dormant. Does best facing south or west.

Parthenocissus (Virginia creeper) A very strong climber with beautiful leaves suffused brilliant red and crimson in autumn. *P. henryana* colours magnificently before leaf fall. Self clinging, will grow in sun or shade in all aspects. However, autumn coloration is best when full light falls upon the leaves so for preference avoid north aspect.

Polygonum baldschuanicum (Russian vine, mile-a-minute vine) A really tough and fast growing deciduous climber, will grow about 5 m (16 ft) in a single season. Will stand hard pruning, twine around anything and grow in the most inhospitable places. Covered from July to October with a froth of loose panicles of flowers faintly tinted pink.

Pyracantha atalantioides (firethorn) Bears masses of white flowers in spring, brilliant crimson fruits the size of peas from November to late February. Of very neat habit, is easily trained against a wall. Has narrow pointed leaves 2.5–5 cm (1–2 in) and thorns about 2 cm (1 in) long; branches too are often thorn tipped. Other useful varieties: *P. angustifolia* (orange berries; south or west aspect) and *P. crenulata* 'Flava' (brilliant yellow berries).

Rosa Roses can be grown as climbers or ramblers on walls, pillars, pergolas and fences providing you select the right variety for the site. You can create superb effects as long as the colour of your roses does not clash with the background. (See pages 83–87 for more detailed information on the planting and care of roses.) Everblooming Climbers flower all summer and carry fair sized blooms Try 'Copenhagen' (bright red) and 'Royal Gold' (deep yellow). Among the Rambling Roses try 'Albertine' (copper shading pink), 'American Pillar' (red with a white eye), 'Paul's Scarlet Climber' (very free and vigorous).

Wisteria Likes good loamy soil; a sunny position is essential. *W. sinensis* has mauve/purple flowers of great fragrance in trusses up to 25 cm (10 in). Grow it on a laburnum tree for a most attractive combination when they are both in flower. *W. venusta* has flowers which are larger and white, but with little if any scent. Both varieties flower May/June.

Trees for Town Dwellers

When choosing a tree for the confined area of a town garden you must always take into account the ultimate size to which it will grow. Never plant one which will prevent light reaching your windows or those of your neighbours. Remember that tree roots can damage drains and foundations, and that in autumn leaves can be a real nuisance, blocking roof gutters and fall-pipes. The trees you choose should suit your garden, not dominate it.

Owners of town gardens are often deterred from planting trees because they think they will be letting themselves in for extra work with pruning. This is an unnecessary worry because, far from it being desirable to undertake pruning every year or so, the truth of the matter is that the less you tamper with the tree, unless there is some definite need to do so, the better. Every pruning cut, even though it be sealed, is a potential source of infection. A great deal of the problems such as those described above are a consequence of a tree not having been suitable for a town garden in the first place, so if you have space to plant a tree, check first with the list of suitable trees given below. If, however, you have inherited any tree that has become a nuisance, read the cautionary note at the end of the chapter before attempting to get rid of it yourself.

Planting and staking

Plant deciduous trees between November and March. Where possible complete your planting before the turn of the year so that the roots have time to gain contact with the soil before the buds begin to move. Later planting can leave trees susceptible to spring droughts, and some may subsequently die. Newly planted trees need regular and generous weekly watering. Use a hose and apply the water in the form of a gentle rain, allowing it to soak into the soil and penetrate well below root level.

Evergreens are best planted in the autumn when the soil is warm and moist, or in the spring, and should be handled like evergreen hedges (see pages 90–93).

Diagrams 51a–j illustrate how trees should be planted. Dig a hole large enough for the root ball (see diagram 51a), for the roots must not be cramped. The hole should also be deep enough to plant the tree at the same depth as before. Look for the soil stain on the stem which marks the old ground level.

Fork over the base of the hole and incorporate some leaf mould or other suitable material (see diagram 51b). Knock the stake into the

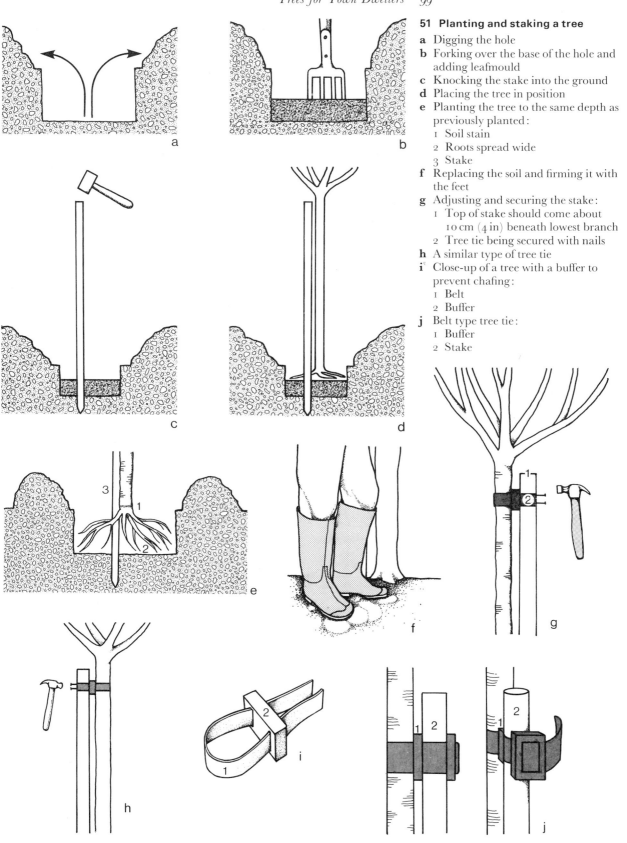

51 Planting and staking a tree

a Digging the hole
b Forking over the base of the hole and adding leafmould
c Knocking the stake into the ground
d Placing the tree in position
e Planting the tree to the same depth as previously planted:
  1 Soil stain
  2 Roots spread wide
  3 Stake
f Replacing the soil and firming it with the feet
g Adjusting and securing the stake:
  1 Top of stake should come about 10 cm (4 in) beneath lowest branch
  2 Tree tie being secured with nails
h A similar type of tree tie
i Close-up of a tree with a buffer to prevent chafing:
  1 Belt
  2 Buffer
j Belt type tree tie:
  1 Buffer
  2 Stake

ground now (see diagram 51c), not after the tree has been planted when it might damage hidden roots. Then place the tree in the hole against the stake, spread out the roots (see diagram 51d) and gradually return the soil (see diagram 51e), working it between the roots and firming it with your feet (see diagram 51f).

The stake should not enter the crown of the tree in case it damages the branches during strong winds. If it is too tall saw the top off so as to leave it some 10 cm (4 in) beneath the lowest branch (see diagram 51g), and finally secure the tree to the stake with a patent tree-tie made of rubber or plastic (see diagrams 51g and 51h). It will usually have a buffer which is positioned between the tree and the stake to prevent chafing (see diagrams 51i and 51j). Tree-ties can be home-made using an old cycle tyre for the buffer and pieces of old leather belt for the strap, which should be nailed to the stake.

Instant trees

Young trees will take several years to reach their full height. If you are not willing to wait you should consider planting semi-mature trees instead, though they may cost 6 to 10 times as much.

There are contractors who specialize in supplying these trees, and they normally agree to replace any which have failed to establish themselves a year after planting. There must of course be some means of access to your garden for the contractor and his equipment.

One point to consider is how you want the contractor to secure your trees. Wire guys running from the tree to pegs in the ground are effective but can be a real nuisance or even a hazard in a small garden. When placing your order you should insist on underground guying, which is a very reliable means of support (see diagram 52).

The best trees for town gardens

The following selection includes some trees which will look well as a backcloth to your garden and others which will make good special features.

Acer palmatum (Japanese maple) 'Dissectum' makes a small shrubby tree about 2 m (6 ft) tall with a low rounded head. The deep-cut bright green foliage turns the most gorgeous shades of orange-yellow and chestnut before leaf fall.

Betula pendula 'Youngii' (weeping birch). One of the most outstanding trees for a small garden, 3.5–4.5 m (11–14 ft) tall with the tips of its branches touching the ground. Its head is dome shaped and both in and out of leaf this tree has an air of majesty.

Cercis siliquastrum (Judas tree) Planted as a shrub about 1 m (3 ft) tall it eventually forms a small tree. Its branches are clustered in purplish rose pea-flowers in late April and May just before the rounded leaves expand. Purple tinted seed pods become conspicuous during August. Likes a warm sunny position and good drainage, and makes an ideal feature on the lawn.

Chamaecyparis lawsoniana (Lawson cypress) 'Columnaris Glauca' is an evergreen of a nice cheerful sea green. A small narrow conical tree with a compact habit it grows to 4 m (13 ft).

Cotoneaster A large family of trees and shrubs some of which are virtually

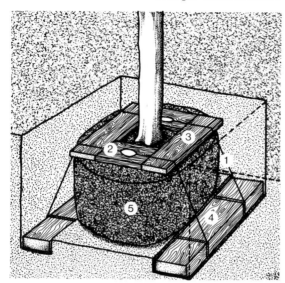

52 A recommended method of underground securing of semi-mature trees; section of a tree pit

1 Guy wire
2 Turnbuckles: these control the tension and can be adjusted if the guys require attention
3 Framework of wooden slats, 15 cm (6 in) by 2.5 cm (1 in)
4 Wooden sleepers
5 Root ball: the top of this must coincide with the existing ground level; regular weekly watering sufficient to reach the depth of the rootball is essential during the growing season throughout the first two seasons after planting; a surface mulching of peat will help to retain soil moisture around the roots

evergreen except during the hardest winter. They have beautiful autumn colours in either foliage or fruit and in spring their branches are smothered with white or pinkish flowers. *C. cornubius* has very large red berries, a somewhat spreading habit, grows to 5.5 m (17½ ft). *C. frigidus* is of small spreading habit, grows to 4.5 m (14 ft), has brilliant red berries. *C. hybridus-pendulus* is evergreen with shiny green foliage, absolutely covered with gorgeous bright red berries during autumn. Makes a small weeping tree 2.5 m (8 ft) high. *C. rothschildianus* has light green willow-like leaves and yellow berries which remain well into winter. Height 4.5 m (14 ft).

Crataegus oxycanthoides (hawthorn, may) 'Paul's Scarlet' is one of the best and flourishes in industrial towns and along windswept shores. When once established is equally tolerant of moist or dry situations. Produces masses of double scarlet flowers in spring and bright red berries in autumn. Has a round head, grows to 5–6 m (16–20 ft).

Fraxinus excelsior 'Pendula' (weeping ash) Fast growing, thrives anywhere and on any type of soil. Grows to only 3 m (10 ft). The flat umbrella-shaped head has branches cascading to the ground in a wide mound.

Laburnum (golden rain) Superb for a small garden, establishing itself fairly rapidly on nearly all types of soil. Best is undoubtedly 'Vossii', very free flowering with long racemes and glossy dark green leaves, producing few of the poisonous seed pods.

Libocedrus decurrens (incense cedar) A very fine, slow-growing evergreen tree, eventually forming a column up to 2 m (6½ ft) wide and 20 m (65 ft) high. Strikingly beautiful with dark green foliage, very much worth planting as a special feature either as a single specimen or in a group for formal effect.

Magnolia Likes deep well-drained fertile soil, a sunny position and shelter from strong winds. Is highly resistant to atmospheric pollution and can be made to flourish even on heavy clay soil provided that plenty of leaf mould or peat is incorporated prior to planting. *M. liliflora* makes a small shrubby tree 3 m (10 ft) high and during April/May has creamy white flowers flushed purple on the outside. *M. soulangeana* is one of the most popular. Varieties include *M.s.* 'Alba Superb' (fragrant white waxy flowers), *M.s.* 'Lennei' (flowers like tulips, rose purple without and white within). Both flower April/May. *M. stellata* displays semi-double white scented flowers during March/April and grows to 2.5 m (8 ft).

Malus (flowering crab apple) Easily grown on any soil, flourishes even in an exposed garden. *M.* 'Almey' displays soft red flowers early in April and retains orange-red fruits until winter. *M.* 'Lady Northcliffe' forms a handsome small tree smothered in pink-white flowers April/May and then in numerous yellow fruits.

Nyssa sylvatica (tupelo) A delightful slow growing deciduous tree with dark green leaves in summer which in autumn turn orange, yellow and scarlet.

Prunus This very large family includes some of the most beautiful flowering trees such as cherries, plums, almonds, peaches, apricots and several laurels. They all benefit from lime and well drained ground. Good deep cultivation and the incorporation of plenty of organic matter are essential before planting. *P. amygdalus* (common almond) is very hardy, thrives in industrial towns and bears masses of pale pink blossom on naked branches during March regardless of the weather. *P.* 'Fudanzakura' displays single white flowers between November and April in a most spectacular manner. *P.* 'Amanogawa' (Lombardy poplar cherry) is ideal where space is limited. Grows 5–6 m (16–20 ft) yet if planted near the house will not block the light. It is one mass of semi-double pink fragrant blossom during April/May.

Pyrus salicifolia 'Pendula' (willow leaf pear). A delightful small weeping form with leaves covered in silky white down until early summer when they turn greyish green.

Creating a sub-tropical atmosphere

With the aid of certain shrubs and trees you can give the impression that your particular garden is especially favoured by the sun.

Cordyline australis (cabbage palm) A small evergreen tree about 3.5 m (11 ft) high with masses of long narrow leaves up to 60 cm (2 ft) long coming away from the top of the trunk. It is quite hardy in sheltered localities but if your area suffers from severe winter frosts or the cold north-east wind, grow it in a large container so that it can be moved to a more sheltered spot in winter. This restricts growth but may keep the tree small enough to install it in a cold greenhouse or garage. (See diagram on page 114.)

Eucalyptus (gum tree) A large genus of fast growing evergreens with distinctive blue-green soft foliage, well adapted to a wide range of soil conditions. *E. coccifera* (Mount Wellington peppermint) has strikingly blue foliage and stems and can withstand severe winter conditions. *E. gunnii* (cider gum) is fairly hardy but needs some protection during the first couple of years. Erect a wattle or hessian screen on the windward side before the onset of winter. The young foliage is rounded and silvery blue while in mature trees it is sickle shaped and greyish blue. *E. niphophila* (snow gum) is perhaps one of the hardiest, a very attractive small tree of slow growth with glaucous foliage and grey peeling bark.

Trachycarpus fortunei (Chusan palm) A decorative tree with large fan-shaped leaves which persist for many years and a trunk thickly covered with the fibrous remains of old stems. Flourishes quite freely in the south and west, but further north keep it sheltered.

Yucca A distinctive shrub with rosettes of sword-like evergreen leaves of tropical appearance, surmounted during July/August with flowering spikes of creamy or white flowers. Not completely hardy in all parts of the country but will grow satisfactorily in sunny conditions on well drained soil. In cold districts with severe frosts it needs a little shelter. *Y. filamentosa* is stemless with a dense clump of erect glaucous leaves 60 cm (2 ft) long. The spike is 90–180 cm (3–6 ft) high, consisting of a large number of yellowish white flowers. *Y. gloriosa* is tree-like with a stout stem, about 2 m (6 ft) high. The glaucous green leaves are very stiff and the flowers creamy white, occasionally tinged with red, packed closely on the conical inflorescence 1–2 m (3–6 ft) high. (See diagram on page 114.)

Woodman, spare that tree

A word of caution before you're tempted to take an axe to a tree in your garden, in order to make more space or to let in light and air. Don't be in too much haste to tackle the job. The do-it-yourself tree feller can be heading for big trouble. He can wreck his own property or someone else's in the attempt—and he might even kill himself in the process. Tree felling is a job for the tree surgeon, who has the equipment, the skill and also the insurance cover. Trying to save money on this job could be false economy if you end up paying for the damage to your neighbour's greenhouse. Before deciding on any action whatsoever, check with your local Parks Department. The tree may be the subject of a preservation order and if this is the case you would have to submit details of what you propose to do, and this work could not be undertaken without the local authorities' consent first being granted. You would be well advised to be clear about such obligations before starting to fell a tree or commissioning someone else to do so, because it could lead to legal problems. So make sure you know where you stand right from the start.

The Urban Water Garden

Water fascinates most people, and many feel that a garden is not complete without a water feature. The tranquil sound of a playing fountain or the murmur of a waterfall attracts birds, and a pond provides a home for fish and a place for growing water lilies. No garden is too small to accommodate a pool of some sort.

A word of warning, however. If there are young children about a pool is a pleasure it would be wise to postpone, because the risk of a toddler drowning in even shallow water is a very real hazard. Don't forget, too, that your neighbours' children will be at risk unless you maintain your hedges or fences in a childproof condition. It is possible to make a pool safe for small intruders, but protective netting or metal grilles detract greatly from its appearance.

Choosing a site

You may want to set your pool into the lawn, raise it slightly as a feature in a rockery, or incorporate it in a patio. Whatever you decide, make sure it is in a sunny position, for water lilies and most aquatic plants will not flourish in the shade.

Try to avoid siting a pool close to trees, for in the autumn decaying leaves in the water will use up all the available oxygen, killing both fish and plant life. The only solution is to place a net over the water as soon as the leaves begin to fall. Tree roots can also cause leaks in the pool lining as they search for water.

Plastic lined and fibreglass pools

By far the cheapest and easiest way to construct a pool is to make an excavation of the required shape and size and simply line it with polythene. This material has a life expectancy of only 2 to 3 years so to prevent sudden leaks it is wise to reline such pools every second year. Use good strong polythene—the 500 gauge kind.

PVC sheeting is far more durable, and reinforced PVC sheeting, which is more expensive, will last for years as long as you leave it undisturbed. Polythene and PVC can easily be pierced, so if you have this type of pool make a firm family rule: *no poking about in the pool with sticks*.

The top edge of a pool must be level on all sides, otherwise it will look most peculiar when it is filled with water. Use a straight-edge and a spirit level when pegging out the area and keep checking as the work proceeds. No part of the pool should be more than 50 cm (20 in) deep when

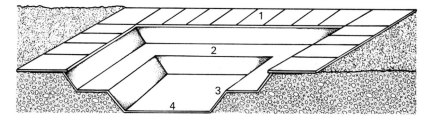

53 A section through a PVC garden pool

1 Paving stones
2 Plant shelf
3 Excavation lined with sand
4 PVC sheeting

completed, and ledges 40 cm (16 in) wide and 22 cm (9 in) deep should be created around the sides for marginal plants. The sides above and below the ledges should slope slightly. (See diagram 53.)

Formal shapes are easier to create than asymmetrical ones, though when using a plastic lining the material is simply pressed into the chosen shape, however irregular, by the sheer weight of the water when the pool is filled.

In any soil other than the most sandy of stone-free loams you would be well advised to remove 5 cm (2 in) of earth beyond the depths recommended above and replace it with fine sand, or soil passed through a fine sieve, to make a nice soft cushion on which the pool liner may be bedded. If the soil or sand is too dry to stay in position you can lightly dampen it from a watering can fitted with a fine rose. You will now be quite certain that no sharp stones can pierce the liner.

To check that the lining material is big enough to cover the bottom and sides of the pool, use a linen tape measure. Start the tape on the ground 30 cm (12 in) beyond the length of the pool. Then let it fall and follow the configuration of the excavation until it reaches the other end, adding a further 30 cm (12 in) there. Do the same to measure the breadth. When your pool is finished the 30 cm (12 in) overlap of plastic should be made secure by paving stones, which should protrude a little over the water.

Fibreglass pools are available in various sizes and shapes. All you have to do is excavate the shape and, with the aid of a straight-edge and spirit level, ensure that your pool lies perfectly level. A waterfall can be created using a set of three pools as shown in the illustration (see diagram 54).

Concrete pools

Relatively few garden pools are made of concrete nowadays for they are expensive, difficult to construct, and never ready for immediate use because the lime in the concrete is always given out into the water during the first few months, which is detrimental to both fish and plants. You can overcome this problem by filling the pool with water and leaving it to stand for about 4 months to allow time for the lime to escape. Then empty the pool completely, rinse it out with clean water and fill it ready for use.

How to stock your pool

Water lilies do best in still water warmed by the heat of the sun. A fountain constantly throws the water into the air, keeping it relatively cold. In short, fountains and water lilies are best not planned for the same pool unless it is large enough to place the fountain at one end and the water lilies at the other. Other aquatic plants do not pose the same problem, nor do ornamental fish.

A correctly stocked pool does not need any regular attention once

54 A three-tiered water feature

A set of three fibreglass pools used in a
most attractive arrangement. Two of the
smaller pools are set into an earth bank so
that the water can cascade down into the
third large pool set at ground level; this
lower pool contains a small pump which
pumps the water up to the top again. The
raised bank not only provides the height
for a romantic waterfall but lends interest
to a flat town garden—and could serve a
third purpose of concealing the compost
heap or other working area
1 Earth bank
2 Water pump

established apart from an annual tidy up and the removal of dead leaves.
It should contain enough submerged oxygenating plants to ensure a
proper balance between the plant and fish life. The plants absorb the
carbon dioxide breathed out by the fish, and return oxygen to the water.
The fish breathe in the oxygen and use the plants as food and as a
spawning ground, and also control various insects which would otherwise
attack the plants. They also prevent gnats and mosquitoes breeding on
the water. Water snails will help to keep the water clean by eating algae
and acting as general scavengers.

Oxygenating plants can be obtained from garden centres or horticul-
tural stores. The number required depends on the size of the pool; the
supplier will advise you. He will also have all the other bits and pieces for
building and stocking a pool, such as electric fountains, pumps, lights,
fish and fish food. Most of the electrical equipment is available in kit form
with easy to follow instructions.

Goldfish normally survive our winters and they breed readily. They
are usually red but individuals may be yellow or silver or a combination
of these colours. Other good pond fish include the shubunkin, comet
goldfish, golden orfe and golden rudd.

In a particularly severe winter, to prevent the pool freezing solid right
to the bottom, put a few sacks on the surface of the ice. Fish can survive
low temperatures but as a safeguard against their becoming frozen solid,
keep a hole open in the ice (see diagram 55).

55 Protecting the pool in severe winter conditions

1 Sacks placed on the surface to prevent
   water freezing solid
2 Hole in the ice to be kept open when
   there are fish in the pond

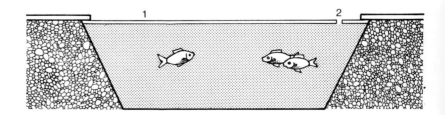

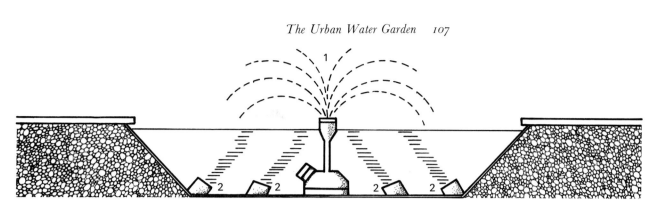

How to plant water lilies

When provided with still warm water and an open sunny situation, water lilies are easy plants to grow. Many are hardy and need no protection during the winter. When well established they will flower all summer, and the more the sun shines the more flowers there will be.

Special moulded plastic containers are available for planting water lilies. Fill them three-quarters full with ordinary garden soil and plant the lilies directly into the soil, taking care not to bury the crowns below it (see diagram 57). Then add a layer of pebbles or gravel to anchor the lilies and prevent the fish from clouding the water by disturbing the soil.

In a single depth pool (see diagram 58a) you will need to support the containers on bricks at first so that the water is no more than 8 cm (3 in) deep above the crowns. As the plants grow the supports can be removed (see diagram 58a). In a two depth pool the container can be placed initially on the shelving (see diagram 58b).

Recommended varieties of water lily

Water lilies vary in the depth of water the full grown plants require. Some of the less vigorous ones will only be happy on the marginal shelf of the pool.

WHITE
Nymphaea 'Albatross' The white lily with golden stamens so frequently portrayed on calendars. Depth 25–60 cm (10–24 in).

56 Possibilities of a single-depth pool
1 Fountain
2 Underwater lighting to add a touch of magic by night

57 Planting a plastic container
1 Three-quarter fill the container with garden soil and plant directly into this
2 Surface the soil with pebbles; keep the crowns of the plants slightly above the surface of the pebbles

58 Planting your pool
a In a single-depth pool you will need to stand the newly planted containers on bricks; later the bricks can be removed
b Start the containers first on the shelf of a two-depth pool

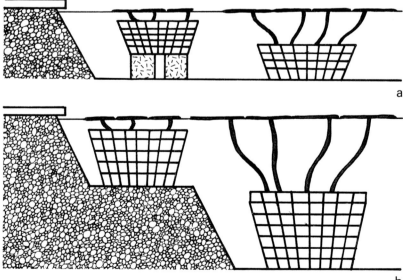

a

b

N. 'Gladstoniana' Large cup-shaped flowers of purest white and shiny bright yellow stamens. Depth 25–60 cm (10–24 in).

N. 'Marliacea Albida' Smaller growing but otherwise similar to 'Albatross'. Depth 20–40 cm (8–16 in).

PINK AND ROSE

N. 'Colossea' Large pink flowers in abundance, turning white with age. Depth 22–80 cm (9–32 in).

N. 'Lustrous' Rose pink flowers with a silvery sheen; very freely flower bearing. Depth 25–60 cm (10–24 in).

N. 'Masaniello' Sweet scented rose-pink peony-shaped flowers produced in abundance over a long season. Depth 25–60 cm (10–24 in).

N. 'Mrs Richmond' Large deep pink flowers becoming an even richer shade in the centre as they mature. Depth 25–60 cm (10–24 in).

N. odorata 'Rosea' An abundance of beautiful rose-pink highly scented flowers. Depth 30–75 cm (12–30 in).

RED AND CRIMSON

N. 'Attraction' Garnet-red flowers shading to deep red, with prolific white sepals. Depth 30–60 cm (12–24 in).

N. 'Ellisana' Good for the smaller pond; glowing red. Depth 15–45 cm (6–18 in).

N. 'James Brydon' One of the most suitable for the small to medium pond. Produces cup shaped flowers of a rich carmine red in great abundance; will tolerate slight shade. Depth 25–60 cm (10–24 in).

N. 'Newton' Brilliant cherry-red star shaped flowers with bright yellow stamens, often held clear of the water. Depth 25–60 cm (10–24 in).

YELLOW AND COPPER

N. 'Aurora' The small flowers are yellow when they first open but later turn deep apricot and finally dark red. Foliage mottled. Depth 10–25 cm (4–10 in).

N. 'Indiana' Flowers are very changeable, opening pale reddish orange but later dark coppery red. Foliage mottled. Depth 25–50 cm (10–20 in).

N. odorata 'Sulphurea Grandiflora' Deep star-shaped yellow flowers held clear of the water; may remain open in the evening. Depth 25–60 cm (10–24 in).

N. 'Sunrise' Undoubtedly the best of the yellow water lilies for colour, fragrance, and size of flowers, which may be anything up to 30 cm (12 in) in diameter. Depth 20–60 cm (8–24 in).

Marginal plants
No garden pool is complete without at least a few plants growing in the shallow water around the edge or on damp ground close by.

Acorus calamus variegatus Very striking leaves striped green and cream. Height 60 cm (24 in). Depth 8–13 cm (3–5 in).

Butomus umbellatus (flowering rush) A rush-like stem with heads of rose pink flowers in May/July. Height 75 cm (30 in). Depth 8–13 cm (3–5 in).

Caltha palustris plena (double kingcup) A great asset to any pool. Produces an abundance of yellow flowers April/June. Height 15 cm (6 in). Depth 1 cm ($\frac{1}{2}$ in).

Cyperus longus (sweet galingale, ornamental rush) Much sought after by flower arrangers for its graceful chestnut-brown plumes. Height 90 cm (36 in). Depth 8–13 cm (3–5 in).

Eriophorum angustifolium (cotton grass) Slender stems and plumes of shining silvery white. Height 30–35 cm (12–14 in). Depth 1 cm ($\frac{1}{2}$ in).

Glyceria spectabilis variegata Prominently variegated leaves striped green, yellow and white; some pink tinting in spring and autumn. Height 60 cm (24 in). Depth $2\frac{1}{2}$–5 cm (1–2 in).

Iris kaempferi (Japanese clematis-flowered iris) Equally at home just in the water or close by its edge. Includes shades of white, blue, violet, purple and plum red. 'Higo Mixed' is the one to choose for a real show of colour with double flowers up to 25 cm (10 in) in diameter. Height 45 cm (18 in).

Lysichitum americanum (skunk lily) Beautiful yellow flowers with an unpleasant odour appear in April. The abundant foliage develops after the flowers. Needs planting in moist soil by the water's edge. Height 90 cm (36 in).

Pontederia cordata (pickerel) Blue flowers closely packed on a spike rather like a small delphinium, July/August. Height 45 cm (18 in). Depth 8–13 cm (3–5 in).

Sagittaria japonica plena (arrowhead) Arrow shaped leaves and fully double white flowers in June/July. Height 60 cm (24 in). Depth 10 cm (4 in).

Scirpus lacustris (true bulrush) Tall slender dark-green stems. Height 120 cm (47 in). Depth 5–10 cm (2–4 in).

Veronica beccabunga Vivid blue flowers and shiny dark green foliage. Height 15 cm (6 in). Depth 0–4 cm (0–$1\frac{1}{2}$ in).

Solutions for Problem Corners

In many town gardens there are spots where everything you plant seems to fail, even after you have done your best with normal cultivation and fertilizers. However, there is no need to despair. First consider what can be done to improve the basic conditions. If there is heavy shade, can you cut back any plants to allow more light in? If masses of tree roots are feeding on the soil, would you cause any serious damage by removing some of them? If the soil is wet, introduce coarse sand or power station ash, if this happens to be available in your area, to improve the drainage. Where it is hard and stony, importing some topsoil might help.

When you have done what you can to the soil, choose some acceptable type of planting material which will at least hide the ground from view.

Shrubs for ground cover

Note that for quick coverage of the ground the smaller shrubs should be planted not more than 30 cm (12 in) apart in each direction.

Aucuba japonica Both spotted and green varieties can deal with most conditions. Height 2–4 m (6–12 ft).

Bergenia cordifolia Short and very hardy with handsome evergreen foliage and, during March/April, deep pink flowers in dropping sprays on stems 25–30 cm (10–12 in) tall.

Cotoneaster horizontalis (fish bone cotoneaster) Ideal for banks and flat ground. Can also be planted against walls. The branches spread horizontally fan-wise and only slowly upwards, with bright red berries in autumn. Does well in the poorest soil but must have some sun. Height 60 cm (24 in).

Euonymus radicans A dense evergreen about 30 cm (12 in) tall which spreads by creeping along the ground. Thrives in dense shade or sun, and if given a wall space easily climbs to a height of 5–6 m (16–20 ft). Old plants can be very rapidly propagated. Simply pull off small pieces and stick them in the soil.

Hebe 'Pagei' An excellent evergreen ground coverer with glaucous grey foliage, bearing quantities of small white flowers May/June. Height 15–23 cm (6–9 in).

Hedera helix (common ivy) One of the most reliable plants in dense shade. The small-leaved varieties look best in such places.

Hypericum patulum 'Hidcote' A semi-evergreen, will thrive in any well drained soil in full sun or partial shade. Of a close compact habit, bears masses of golden yellow flowers from July to October. Height 1.2 m (3½ ft).

Mahonia aquifolium (Oregon grape, holly leafed berberis) Evergreen, excellent ground cover under trees. The polished green holly-like leaves often have blood red patches in winter. Produces broad golden yellow flower spikes in spring and later very attractive blue black berries. Height 1–2 m (3–5 ft).

Rhododendron ponticum Flourishes in heavy shade and relatively poor soil. Evergreen, producing lots of mauve to lilac pink flowers in May/June. In somewhat confined spaces prune every 2 years and remove some of the growing points yearly. Full height 4–6 m (12–20 ft).

Ruscus hypoglossum This evergreen dwarf shrub forms broad clumps with green leafy stems carrying inconspicuous green flowers. Female plants produce large cherry red fruits. Likes dry shady places and all types of soil. Maximum height 45 cm (18 in).

Symphoricarpos albus (common snowberry) A quite hardy deciduous shrub with slender erect shoots in a dense clump. Grows well in shade on all types of soil and among the roots of trees. Flowers are relatively insignificant but are followed in autumn by white berries. Height about 2 m (5–7 ft).

Vinca major (greater periwinkle) A spreading ground cover shrub with glossy dark green foliage and large blue flowers from late April to June and again September/October. Ideal for banks and for awkward spots in sun or shade. Height 30 cm (12 in).

Vinca minor (lesser periwinkle) Grows to about 20 cm (8 in) but flowering period is the same as *Vinca major*. Forms an extensive carpet even in dense shade.

Back Yards, Courtyards and Patios

Many town gardeners have no open earth at all to work on, but only concrete—perhaps a tiny back yard surrounded by blank high walls. Courtyards provide a bit more space, and patios may or may not have an adjoining garden. But in all three cases the problem is the same: how to soften the appearance of the hard surfaces without using up too much space.

Start with the walls and fences

If you have high walls like a prison yard your first step is to get out a large distemper brush and paint them a brilliant white, to reflect as much light as possible and make a good background for your flowers.

An ugly chain link fence can be concealed with a creeper for beauty and privacy. If there is a narrow gap of soil you could plant the 'mile-a-minute vine' (see page 97). This fast-growing climber will lose all its leaves during the winter but in time its twiggy stems will so twine about that it will almost resemble a wattle fence. If you prefer an evergreen, consider an ivy such as *Hedera canariensis* (see page 96), though ivy does not grow nearly so quickly. If you are really impatient the answer may be to put up wovenboard fencing panels.

On the back walls of the house you can train suitable creepers such as *Clematis*, *Hedera* or *Parthenocissus*, all of which will grow happily even on a north-facing wall (see pages 96–97). Don't cover every wall with climbers; use just enough to break the hard surfaces.

The view from the house

How can you improve the outlook from your windows? You can secure window boxes immediately outside them (see pages 77–80) but you should also take into account the full length of the yard. What can be done with this area while still leaving enough room to stroll about? A back wall which has had a good coat of Snowcem has great potential. Consider putting up some hanging baskets; their flowers would provide a fine display against the white background.

You could place a large flower trough against the end wall, but make sure that outbuildings do not obscure your view of it. To be seen easily from inside the house the trough should be raised by about 30 cm (12 in). Make it a good length to accommodate both annual bedding and several permanent shrubs such as dwarf conifers. Consider its relationship to any hanging baskets so that together they will form a good composite feature.

a

b

c

59 The mobile garden

Casters enable heavy containers to be moved to suit the sun, the season and your own convenience; they are quite serviceable provided they are oiled occasionally

a Wooden tub mounted on cross members bearing casters

b and c A simple trolley makes it easy to move large containers of clay or rigid polythene

If you have only a low wall or fence different solutions will have to be considered. If your yard is paved rather than solid concrete you may be able to remove the occasional paving slab so that the hardcore can be excavated down to the soil and then topped up with good quality topsoil. Then you could plant ornamental trees or vigorous shrubs (see pages 98–103). Perhaps you could erect rustic poles (at intervals of 2–3 m or 6–10 ft) and train rambling roses up them. Wistaria is also worthy of serious consideration; the poles for it should be set at intervals of 3 m (10 ft) and a strong metal cable should be strained across the tops.

Movable plants

If you cannot plant anything directly into the soil you can still grow shrubs and small trees in tubs. If you put the tubs on casters they may be pushed aside when more space is needed and you can keep the most prominent position filled by whichever plant is currently the most attractive.

It is easy to fix two cross members of timber to the bottom of wooden tubs, but take care not to obstruct the drainage holes. The casters are then screwed to the cross members (see diagram 59a). If you are using stone, plastic or earthenware containers (see diagrams 59c and 59d), construct a shallow trolley on casters to fit underneath them (see diagram 59b). A large flower box becomes much more mobile if you equip it with casters (see diagram 60). Oil the casters occasionally.

Courtyards of character

If you are fortunate enough to have a courtyard the possibilities are considerable. It will certainly have some atmosphere of its own from the

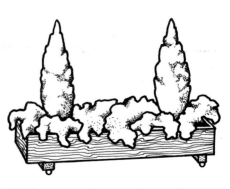

60 Casters make even a heavy flower box mobile

61 A tropical atmosphere for your courtyard—construct a well and surround it with large clay containers growing exotic-looking plants

1 Kentia palm
2 *Cordyline australis*
3 *Yucca gloriosa*

outset. Paving or cobblestones, existing trees or the shape of the buildings will help you to arrive at a design solution which will be aesthetically satisfying and at the same time functional.

Select the most desirable place for a sitting-out area. What about a water feature? Cascading fountains add a Spanish flavour. A small well could be constructed in the same material as the buildings, complete with its iron framework and bucket. A tropical effect can be created, perhaps around the well (see pages 102–103 and diagram 61). Window boxes, troughs, tubs and climbers will all have their particular place.

Floodlighting can do wonders for confined city gardens, making them more attractive during the warmer evenings and creating an enchanting scene at night by picking out the special features.

Perfect patios

Most patios are an extension of your living area, contiguous with the house on one side and possibly marrying up with a garden on the other. Several tubs of shrubs on casters might be a good idea, but if they take up too much space you could confine any containers to the corners. An old barrow will make a very simple and attractive container for a bedding display (see diagram 62).

The best arrangement might be window boxes plus a small area of formal garden or a flower border on the garden side of the patio. Dwarf conifers of various sorts can be interspersed with summer bedding, and winter flowering primulas can be plunged into the border. Spring flowering bulbs can also be planted. A *Camellia japonica* planted at one side of the border does not interfere with the summer display but can be appreciated from the house while it is flowering in late winter and early spring. Hanging baskets will cheer the place up without detracting from its more functional purpose.

Wistaria or climbing roses can be trained to cover the walls. Where the patio has steps leading down to a garden you might flank them with pots or tubs of annual bedding plants or suitable evergreens for year round interest.

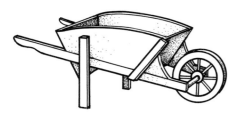

62 A bedding display in an old barrow looks pretty in its prime—and can be replanted or simply moved out of sight once the summer flowers are over

Gardens in the Clouds

Many town gardens can be considerably enlarged by using a little bit of initiative. Inspect the outside of your house or flat. Are there balconies? Flat parts on the roof? What about the garage roof? Are there any other projections to your property? If you possess any spaces like these you can probably build a roof garden.

Before you launch out on detailed plans there are three questions which must be answered satisfactorily:

Will the roof bear the weight of a garden?
Can you shelter it from the wind?
Can you arrange for a convenient water supply?

The structure of the roof

Make a close inspection of your proposed site. If the roof is of pre-stressed concrete then you have a perfect location. If it is made of lead, or of a lightweight material with a bituminous surface, which is more likely with older town property, you will have to be more ingenious in developing it. Its weight-bearing potential will not be very great; you may even have to be careful when walking about on it.

With lightweight roofs you must be quite certain that the timber or metal structure underneath is sound, and if you are in doubt about this seek professional advice before going any further. When you are satisfied on this score you should provide a slatted wooden deck preserved with Cuprinol. (See diagram 63a.) This will make a safe walk-way, preserve the roof from damage, aid considerably with weight distribution, and solve the drainage problem.

Shelter from the wind

Wind is always a problem with roof gardens. Stand on the site of the garden and look about you. Are there any surrounding walls which already form windbreaks? Are there high-rise blocks nearby? These create ferocious downdraughts. From which direction does the prevailing wind blow? Most important of all, which way does your site face? Will it provide a suntrap suitable for a sitting-out area?

You may have to build some form of sheltering wall, but be careful about cutting off the light from the south and west, as this may create undue shading. Never build shelter walls on all four sides, for when the wind blows strongly you will have a whirlpool of air, and the higher the

63 Spreading the load

a 1 Reinforced PVC sheeting supports the soil-less compost
  2 A slatted wooden deck will help to preserve the roof from damage and solve the drainage problem
  3 Planking as support along the front of borders
  4 Second piece of planking placed at the point where two lengths of the planking meet—see bird's eye view below
  5 Container to hold planks in place
  6 *Thuya zebrina plicata*, a suitable conifer for the roof garden
b Bird's eye view:
  1 Reinforced PVC sheeting
  2 Soil-less compost
  3, 4 Planking
  5 Container
c Border for a concrete roof:
  1 Reinforced PVC sheeting
  2 Soil-less compost
  3 Flower box supporting timber

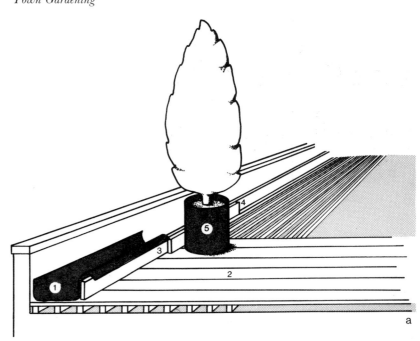

a

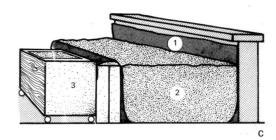

b

c

walls the worse it will be. The best solution is a screen on no more than two sides, preferably made of a trellis which will support climbing plants. Around a sitting-out area you can make the screen more windproof by building into it sheets of transparent PVC or closely-bound split bamboo screening.

The water supply

Roof gardens need quite a lot more water than similar areas at ground level, for the wind dries the compost out very quickly. Carrying water to the site by hand can become so irksome that it takes all the pleasure out of the project. So install a tap on the roof, remembering to insulate the pipe well. Then attach a hose to water your plants, or use sprinkler-type hoses which will do the job by themselves as soon as the tap is turned on.

Tubs and flower beds

Most planting in a roof garden should be confined to containers made of lightweight materials. Earthenware and stone receptacles should only be used where the roof is of reinforced concrete. In any case, keep tubs and borders as far as possible near the edges of the roof, next to the strong outer walls. (See diagrams 64 and 65.) You can be a little more liberal with borders when the roof is of concrete.

For bedding, first put down a sheet of reinforced PVC (see diagram 63*a*).

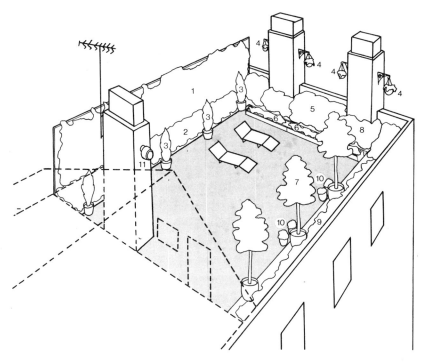

64 Features for a roof garden

This design illustrates the basic principle to be followed when planning any roof garden—the weight of the plants and compost must be distributed around the edges of the roof adjacent to the outer walls:

1 Screen fence on which the Russian vine, *Polygonum baldschuanicum* is growing
2 Herbaceous border
3 Large conifers
4 Hanging baskets
5 Suitable site for a few shrubs
6 Flower boxes for spring and summer bedding
7 Swedish birch, *Betula pendula dalecarlica*
8 *Clematis* 'Nelly Moser'
9 Rose border
10 Plants in portable containers
11 Floodlights so roof garden can be used on mild evenings

65 Making the maximum use of a modest roof space

1 *Wisteria sinensis*
2 *Robinia pseudoacacia* 'Frisia'
3 Conifers
4 *Cotoneaster cornubia*
5 Flower boxes for spring and summer flowers

Turn the edges of the sheet upwards and inwards to support the compost. Keep the sides in place with lengths of Cuprinol-preserved timber and support the ends with boxes of plants. Puncture tiny holes across and along the sheet to aid drainage. On top of this place one of the lightweight soil-less composts such as J. Arthur Bowers' or Levington. These are excellent growing mediums but are much lighter than soil. (See diagrams 63b and 63c.)

Planning for your plants

Providing the roof garden is sheltered from strong winds and receives a reasonable amount of sunlight it will sustain most plants just as well as the ordinary garden on the ground.

Climbers deserve special consideration, for their roots take up little space while they cover large areas of wall and trellis. Trees will grow quite comfortably for 5 to 10 years in large tubs, after which they should be removed to a natural garden situation. Renew the compost in the tubs and plant new trees in them. Trees and larger shrubs should be well anchored to the roof.

Frost damage is a danger, since the plant roots cannot protect themselves by spreading deeply into soil. If you expect a severe winter place layers of sacking round the containers of the more valuable plants and then cover this with plastic sheeting in order to both keep it dry and preserve the insulation.

Conifers and evergreens are particularly useful, for in winter they provide some shelter for the more tender plants and are an attraction in their own right. In spring and summer they make an excellent backcloth for the flowering plants and shrubs they have helped to protect.

Planning and permission

If you are living in rented property you will have to approach the landlord with your proposals. Before doing so it is as well to have all the details worked out in your mind, for your chances of getting a fair hearing and a positive response will be infinitely better. I would suggest, therefore, that you study diagrams 64 and 65 as these give a clear indication of what can be achieved, and ponder all the points in this chapter before taking any action.

Extra features

Where there is room you can have a small fountain or perhaps even a waterfall. A water feature set among the plants will give the whole garden that extra finishing touch. Pick a suitable place for a sun lounger, or perhaps a couple of garden chairs and a small table. There may be room for a cold frame.

If the space is fairly extensive a far more elaborate design is possible, with a greenhouse or summerhouse, a larger planted area of trees, shrubs and bedding plants, and even a lawn, formal water garden or small swimming pool. But of course such a garden as this would call for considerable building operations and a strong supporting house structure. There are endless possibilities if you have the money and the space.

Pruning: the How and When

First of all we ought to differentiate between the words 'shrub' and 'tree'. A shrub forms a framework of branches near the ground while a tree builds up a strong branch system on the top of a main stem or 'trunk'. Although this is a nice easy generalisation it is not all encompassing: there are variations in the manner of growth and in many cases the demarcation line is unclear.

The natural way

Pruning is a general name used to describe the removal by cutting of any part of a shrub or tree whether it be stem, branch or root. In nature this process has been going on since the beginning of time, for in severe winters the branches of trees and shrubs are killed if they are not hardy enough to stand up to the prevailing conditions. Disease and insect pests can also destroy branches (and indeed entire shrubs and trees). Other, so called, natural means of pruning are physical disorders, for example changes in the level of the water table in the soil and in soil level around the roots or chemical deficiencies in the soil. Nature's way of pruning is not suitable for town gardens or indeed for the nurseryman producing trees and shrubs. It is random, unpredictable and unsightly and this is why man steps in to do a more thorough and satisfactory job.

Reasons for pruning

These are many and varied but the more obvious are as follows:

To remove dead and diseased wood.

To give a shrub or tree some shaping during its formative years.

To restrict growth where space is limited, or to stimulate more vigorous growth.

To allow light to gain entry and air to circulate more freely.

To correct malformation.

To prevent a tree or shrub blocking light from house windows.

To stimulate the flowers, fruit or foliage for which a tree or shrub is being cultivated.

A cautious approach

It is easy, when pruning, to do more harm than good: untold damage to shrubs and trees is caused annually by reckless pruning. Examples abound and you should be certain not to add to that number. Ornamental shrubs and trees, for instance, should be pruned so that their

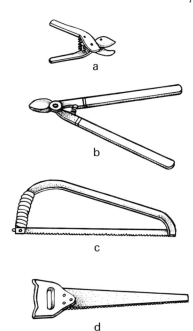

66 Tools for the job

a Secateurs
b Bush pruner
c Bow saw
d Rip saw

67 How to prune trees

a Thin branches can be removed with a bush pruner
b Large heavy branches should be removed in stages with a saw
  1 At each stage the branch should first be undercut until the saw begins to bind. If you saw from above first, the weight of the branch will tear it off and possibly cause damage to the tree
  2 Make a cut from above a little beyond the undercut. The weight of the branch will complete the operation but leave a rough edge
  3 The final stub should be sawn approximately parallel to the trunk to leave a smooth edge
  4 Coat all pruning wounds over 5 cm (2 in) in diameter with a proprietary, fungicidal, waterproof sealant

68 Reason for pruning

Pruning may be necessary to prevent your shrubs and trees obstructing the pavement.

69 Pruning a ground cover shrub

The shrub *Hypericum calycinum* is an example of a ground cover shrub which needs to be cut down with a pair of shears to ground level in early spring.

natural habit and shape are retained. The only exceptions are when shrubs are trained against walls and fences to clothe the surface or when they are being used for topiary work.

If you do decide pruning is necessary, don't rush to buy special tools. Most garden shrubs can be dealt with quite easily using ordinary sécateurs and a small Grecian-type hand saw (see diagram 66a–d). When it comes to pruning ornamental trees, a long arm pruner and a bushman saw will prove adequate. If you belong to a local residents' association or allotments society you will probably be able to borrow any tools you require. The important point to remember is that the tools you are using for pruning must be sharp. All cuts must be made cleanly as crushed wood allows fungal diseases to enter.

When to prune trees

Many people worry without cause about the frequency with which they should prune the trees in the garden. The trees which are most likely to be found in a town garden are those of the forest or ornamental variety. These require no regular pruning programme and should only be touched if they are subject to one of the problems listed above.

Remember that every pruning cut (see diagrams 67a and 67b), even though it be sealed to prevent disease, is a potential source of infection. If in doubt, leave your trees alone until you are able to obtain expert advice on the subject.

When to prune evergreens

Evergreens do not need any regular pruning unless they form part of a formal hedge or screen or are getting too large for their position. Where only one annual clipping of an evergreen hedge is to be made, the best

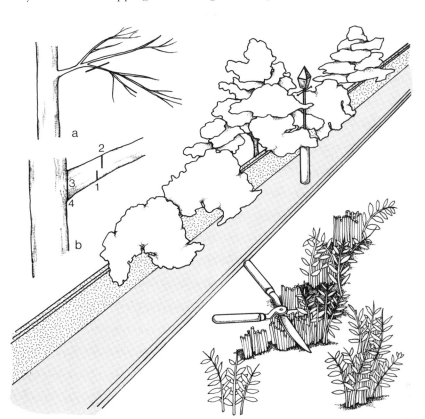

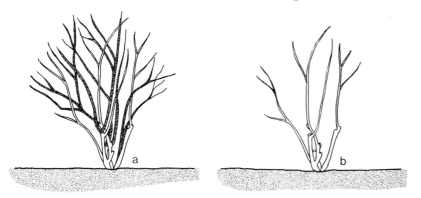

70 How to prune spring-flowering shrubs

Spring-flowering shrubs, such as *Forsythia intermedia 'Spectabilis'*, which produce flowers on shoots of the previous season's growth, should be pruned immediately after the flowers fade. Remove some of the old stems right down to the ground and shorten weak shoots back to strong growth.

a Before pruning
b After pruning

time is during August. If any hard pruning of holly trees is contemplated, this is best undertaken towards the end of April, so that the trees have a full growing season in which to recover from the shock. Other evergreen flowering shrubs, such as *Berberis darwinii* and *Berberis stenophylla*, should have any pruning done immediately the flowers have faded, as should rhododendrons. Autumn-flowering heath such as *Erica tetralix* (cross-leaved heath) and *Erica vagans* (Cornish heath) should be trimmed back in the spring, just before new growth commences; this not only encourages new growth but also assists in keeping the plants compact.

When to prune deciduous shrubs
In general these can be divided into three categories with regard to the time they are best pruned, if indeed any pruning is really necessary.

(1) *Spring-flowering shrubs flowering on shoots produced in the previous year*
Several examples immediately spring to mind – *Forsythia suspensa*, *Jasminum nudiflorum* and *Prunus triloba*. They should all be pruned immediately the flowers fade so they may produce new shoots which will then flower the following year (see diagrams 70a and 70b). If pruning is delayed, it will remove the potential flowering shoots, meaning that there will be precious little flower produced the following spring.

(2) *Shrubs flowering during May, June and July on shoots produced in the previous year*
This category includes *Deutzia*, *Philadelphus*, *Spiraea* and *Weigela*. Prune as soon as flowering is over. The procedure is to remove some of the older worn out flowering shoots, right down to the ground if necessary, to encourage the development of new ones (see diagrams 71a and 71b). Take great care with this kind of pruning technique; over zealousness can result in sacrificing a year's flowering.

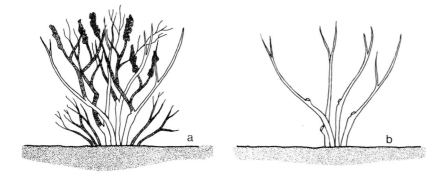

71 How to prune early summer-flowering shrubs

Shrubs which produce flowers in May, June and July on shoots produced in the previous year, such as *Syringa* (lilac) should be pruned by removing the old flowered wood, as the flowers fade, and the occasional stem right down to ground level.

a Before pruning
b After pruning

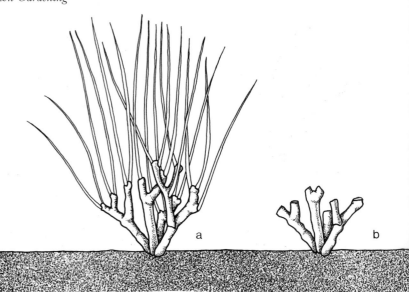

**72 How to prune shrubs flowering on
     shoots produced in the same year**

Shrubs, such as *Buddleia davidii*, which
produce flowers on shoots of the current
year's growth, should be pruned
hard back, almost to the ground, during
early March of each year.
a Before pruning
b After pruning

(3) *Shrubs flowering on shoots produced in the same year*
This category includes such shrubs as *Ceanothus Gloire de Versailles*,
Hibiscus, *Tamarix pentandra* and *Clematis jackmanii*. These should all be cut
back fairly hard, that is to within 6 cm ($2\frac{1}{2}$ in) of the old wood when the
severe weather is over, about February, and weak shoots removed (see
diagrams 72a and 72b).

Getting
Outside Help

The time may come when a job you want done is either beyond your capabilities, or you just can't spare the time for it. How to go about getting in professional help? If all you want is for someone to plant a couple of trees, or half a dozen shrubs, then all you need do is to get one or two quotations over the phone from a garden contractor and place a verbal order with one who comes up with the lowest quote. Make sure that the quotations you obtain are for precisely the same condition, eg, in the case of shrubs and other plants, check whether they are container grown or field grown.

If, however, you want something more ambitious, such as the building of a patio or other major feature, you need to go about it rather more formally, to ensure that you get what you want, that you are not letting yourself in for unforeseen expenditure once the work is in progress, and that the work will be completed in reasonable time. A formal contract is essential if you want to commission some radical alterations such as the professional redevelopment of an old garden.

First set out on paper exactly what you require and get not less than three quotations (invite five and you'll probably get three). The best way to track down suitable garden contractors is to have a word with a senior member of staff of a garden centre on a not too busy day. You may find that the centre is able to undertake the work themselves or if not, they should certainly be able to suggest the name of several competent contractors whose order book is not over-full. At the same time have a look at the materials on display at the centre, ask advice about their durability etc and collect up leaflets relating to any that interest you.

Any contractor who is genuinely interested in the work will certainly want to visit and assess the site before submitting his quotation and obviously it is in your own interest to give him the opportunity. When you receive your quotations, check that the contractor has provided a priced bill of quantities—most do this willingly but some may simply provide you with a gross figure for the whole job. This does not matter if the price is one you feel able to accept but becomes important if you find that all the quotations are higher than you can afford, and you decide to go back to one of the contractors and get him to do a part only of the work for which he has submitted a quote. You may then be able to get the work done in several phases, at later dates in the future, for which revised quotations will be obtainable.

Once you have written to accept a firm quotation, this forms a legally binding contract. Keep your copy of the quotation in case of misunderstanding arising—although when the details are clearly laid out, few problems are likely to arise and any that may can be settled amicably.

Here are some examples of letters and other documents enlisting help from professional garden contractors:

1 SPECIMEN LETTER INVITING QUOTATIONS

Garden Construction & Maintenance,
Brooklands Road,
Kipton.   *19th October, 19 . . . .*

Dear Sir,

I am in the process of inviting quotations for the redevelopment of certain areas of my rear garden at the above address and I wondered if you would like to submit an estimate for the work?

I am enclosing for your information a rough plan showing the area involved, a Specification of Works, a Bill of Quantities and a list of the planting material I require. I would be pleased to arrange for you to view the garden, if you so wish, by prior appointment. Please phone any evening during the week between 6 pm and 7 pm so that we can fix a time to our mutual agreement.

If you wish to be considered for this work will you please be so kind as to write out your tended figure on the enclosed tender form and fill in the other relevant details. Your tender must be returned to me not later than Monday 7th November 19 . . . .

Yours sincerely,

2 EXAMPLE OF A SIMPLE PRIVATE CONTRACT BETWEEN AN INDIVIDUAL AND A LANDSCAPE CONTRACTOR:

Landscape Development Scheme, 13, Walpole Street, Metropolis, WC1 3PL.
Specification of Works:

The contractor commissioned to execute the various works in the rear garden of the above property shall do so to the satisfaction of Mr. J. Clarke. The work entails the partial reconstruction and extension of the garden. The work will include the removal of existing chain link fencing along the south eastern boundary, breaking out of existing paved areas, grubbing out tree stump, dismantling rockery, collecting builders rubble, constructing of crazy paving, gravel path with concrete curbing, construction of a patio with 'Super Style' reconstructed stone, construction of 'Super Style' screen walling along the south eastern and part of the southern boundary, provision of shrubs, the provision of wall creepers, the provision of one tree and the introduction of top soil to the existing flower borders. The contractor is to remove all discarded materials including builders rubble and any other rubbish present in the back garden to his own tip. Care is to be exercised to ensure that none of the existing garden features are damaged as a result of these works. Materials are not to be placed upon the existing lawn area. The contractor will be held responsible to make good at his own expense any damage which may be caused to the garden or adjacent properties during the execution of the various works. The contractor shall leave the garden in a clean and tidy condition when he has completed all the various works.

The various works may commence any time after 2nd January, 19 . . . . but must be completed by 31st March, 19 . . . .

3 EXAMPLE OF A CONTRACTOR'S UNPRICED BILL OF QUANTITIES

Landscape Development Scheme, 13, Walpole Street, Metropolis, WC1 3PL. Bill of Quantities:

		£	P
1	Take down and remove existing chain link fencing.	17.5 m.	
2	Break out all existing paved areas and remove.	60 sq m.	
3	Grub-out tree stump and remove.	Item.	
4	Dismantle rockery and remove stones.	Item.	
5	Remove builders rubble.	8 sq m.	
6	Provide and lay crazy paving.	18 sq m.	
7	Provide and lay gravel path 1.3 m wide in two courses of gravel.	4 cu m.	
8	Hardcore foundation.	2 cu m.	
9	Provide and lay concrete back edging to path.	40 m l.	
10	Provide and lay patio with 'Super Style' reconstructed stone paving.	27.25 sq m.	
11	Hardcore foundation.	6 cu m.	
12	Provide and erect 'Super Style' screen walling consisting of type 3B and 7B pattern blocks in equal numbers to a height of 2 m.	17.5 m l.	
13	Provide and erect 'Super Style' screen walling consisting of type IK pattern blocks to a height of 2 m.	7 m l.	
14	Provide and erect 'Super Style' coping.	24.5 m l.	
15	Provide and erect 'Super Style' piers type IP to a height of 2 m.	9 No.	
16	Provide and erect 'Super Style' pier caps.	9 No.	
17	Hardcore foundation.	4 cu m.	
18	Prepare shrub border.	15 sq m.	
19	Provide and plant assorted shrubs.	20 No.	
20	Provide and plant tree and allow for staking and securing.	Item.	
21	Provide and plant wall creepers.	10 No.	
22	Provide bucket type planters No. 0764.	4 No.	
23	Provide stone planters No. 0137.	3 No.	
24	Provide John Innes Potting Compost No. 2 and fill planters.	7 No.	
25	Construct with turf an extension to existing lawn area.	40 sq m.	

26 Provide and spread top soil to
   flower beds.   2 cu m.

27 Allow for removal of all discarded
   materials and other rubbish to
   contractor's own tip.   Item.

28 Allow for all labour.   Item.

29 Allow for all transport.   Item.

30 Allow for the use of all other
   equipment.   Item

	Total	_____
	VAT	_____
	Grand Total	_____

4 LIST OF PLANTING MATERIAL TO BE SUPPLIED; THIS ACCOMPANIES THE
   BILL OF QUANTITIES

Landscape Development Scheme, 13, Walpole Street, Metropolis, WC1 3PL. List of Planting Material To Be Supplied:

Please note that all the planting material is to be container grown.

		Height	Number
Shrubs:	Buddleia davidii 'Empire Blue'	60–80	3
	Ceanothus 'Gloire de Versailles'	35–45	3
	Cotoneaster horizontalis	35–45	2
	Daphne mezereum	30–40	1
	Eleagnus pungens 'Maculata'	30–40	2
	Hamamelis mollis	35–45	1
	Jasminum officinale	30–40	1
	Magnolia stellata	30–40	1
	Philadelphus microphyllus	30–40	1
	Potentilla fruticosa 'Farreri'	30–40	2
	Senecio 'Greyii'	30–40	1
	Spiraea arguta	45–60	1
	Viburnum rhytidophyllum	40–50	1
Climbers:	Actinidia kolomikta	60–90	1
	Clematis 'Nelly Moser'	75–85	1
	Clematis 'President'	75–85	1
	Clematis 'Ville de Lyon'	75–85	1
	Forsythia suspensa	45–60	1
	Garrya elliptica	30–40	1
	Hedera 'Golden Heart'	45–60	2
	Parthenocissus (Ampelopsis) tricuspidata 'Veitchii'	60–90	1
	Wisteria sinensis	35–45	1
		Metres	
Tree:	Gingo biloba	4–5	1

5 EXAMPLE OF THE CONTRACTOR'S TENDER

To: *Mr. J. Clarke,*
    13, Walpole Street,
    Metropolis, WC1 3PL.   *Date* . . . .

Sir,

    . . . . the undersigned do hereby undertake and agree to execute and complete the whole of the work required at the above address, in accordance with the Specification and Bill of Quantities provided by you. The site has been inspected and all the relevant details checked.

    Firm Price Tender:

. . . . pounds.

. . . . pence.

                        £   P

    Signed . . . .

    Address . . . .

            . . . .

            . . . .

    Telephone Number . . . .

Index